# I Thought I'd Be DONE by Now

## Hope and Help for Mothers of Adult Children Searching for Peace

— VOLUME ONE —

WENDY BOORN, M.C., L.P.C.

I Thought I'd Be Done by Now

Published by Perfect Bound Marketing
Phoenix, Arizona
www.PerfectBoundMarketing.com

Book design by Mullins Creative

ISBN #978-1-939614-01-8

# · Quotes on Motherhood ·

"It kills you to see them grow up.
But I guess it would kill you quicker if they didn't."
~ Barbara Kingsolver

"The mother-child relationship is paradoxical and, in a sense,
tragic. It requires the most intense love on the mother's side, yet
this very love must help the child grow away from the mother
and become independent."
~ Erich Fromm

"Biology is the least of what makes someone a mother."
~ Oprah Winfrey

"Grown don't mean nothing to a mother. A child is a child.
They get bigger, older, but grown? What's that suppose to
mean? In my heart it don't mean a thing."
~ Toni Morrison, *Beloved*, 1987

"Motherhood: All love begins and ends there."
~ Robert Browning

"With what price we pay for the glory of motherhood."
~ Isadora Duncan

"God could not be everywhere, so he created mothers."
~ Jewish Proverb

"But kids don't stay with you if you do it right.
It's the one job where, the better you are,
the more surely you won't be needed in the long run."
~ Barbara Kingsolver

"Mothering never ends; but it
evolves, and our tool boxes need regular overhauls."
~ Wendy Boorn

# · Dedication ·

I dedicate *I Thought I'd Be Done by Now* to ~

Kimberly and Douglas, my beloved children and
muses. Thank you for your support of this project
and for your unconditional love.
Please accept this book as my love letter to you.

My dear mother Margaret Stryke
who inspired me from heaven.

My precious brother, Robert Mieger,
who made his peaceful final transition on the day
this manuscript was completed. I honor Bob as
the kindest soul I ever knew and the most devoted
"mother" a father could be.

# · Table of Contents ·

# · Acknowledgements ·

I began to write *I Thought I'd Be Done by Now* because I was suffering so much anguish about my strained relationship with my daughter. Desperate to gain the understanding and tools needed to preserve and grow that relationship, I began to teach what I needed to learn. Along the way, I realized that I couldn't take this journey alone.

Once I decided to write what would become my first book, I experienced the truth that "when the student is ready, the teacher appears." Many stepped forward to encourage, offer tips and opinions, edit and share their pain. I joined hands with everyone, especially with the many mothers who courageously shared with me their stories of confusion, frustration, heartbreak and, sometimes, of hope and healing. It has been an honor for me to pass their messages along to you, dear readers, and it is my sincere hope that you will be a more effective parent and more at peace after reading these stories.

Deep thanks go to Margaret Winslow, who got the ball rolling; to Brenda Garrett, R.N., L.P.C., who helped me face my need for control; to Mary Westheimer, whose initial support and expertise helped me start typing; to my Bucknell buddies, forever friends for fifty years, for your undying support; to dear friend Marilyn Rampley, who helped me find my title and so much more; to my editor Jackie Dishner, whose conscientious attention to detail, clear and critical eye and ability to "get me" sharpened my message; and to Vickie Mullins and Brandi Hollister, who transformed my manuscript into a book. Finally, my heartfelt thanks to fellow members of the Scottsdale Society of Women Writers — you kept me going by repeatedly telling me to hurry up and publish because you needed my book!

And I send fervent appreciation to my dear friends, colleagues and family, who never lost faith in me, despite the many years it took to complete this project. You contributed stories, read early drafts, voted on book covers, did tasks to free up writing time, wrote blurbs and cheered me on. Included are Meg Allen, Joanne Deck, Robin Dilley, Diane Dillon, Marion Emerson, Carol Gold, Marge Goldstein, Susan Hanson, Mary Herring, Tammie Holt, Beverly Janowitz-Price, Kathy Kane, Elizabeth Keith, Linda Kriesel, Jody Kranz, Anne Lackey, Rachel Loda, Arnold Lopez, Beverly Mahaffey, Sue Meyn, Connie Midey, Judy and Bob Mieger, Arlene Mix, Jane Monachelli, Joyce Murphy, Michele Rechberger, Jenna Ross, Miho

Sasaki, Mike Schelle, Judy Schwiebert, Jane Stidham, Janet Welch, and Julie Yarrow.

*I Thought I'd Be Done by Now* would not exist without the multitude of mothers, as well as some fathers and adult children, who opened their hearts to me. I am truly inspired by their courage and transparency, the expression of which grace these pages. In order to honor their vulnerability, except when given permission to use our conversations as shared, I disguised their identities and the details of their stories. Sometimes, features from two or more stories were combined in one essay. Deep gratitude goes to the following:

Kim A, Ruth A, Susan A, Dee B, Claudia B, Diana B, Kate and Debbie B, Kayleen B, Ken B, Lori B, Lorie B, Mary Ann B, Paula B, Rosemary B, Tricia B, Ben C, Bonnie C, Jacquie C, Laura C, Pamela C, Rhonda C, Ruth C, Penny and Rich D, Debi H, Alice F, Gail F, Joanne G, Mary Dolores G, Michael G, Stephanie G, Suzanne G, Arleen H, Eric and Jan H, Katie H, Rob H and Jill T, Betty J, Cindy and Ted J, Ginger J, Annie K, Joleen L, Karen L, Nancy L, Pam and Stan L-M, Bev M, Cathy M, Johnnie M, Leo M, Molly M, Betsy N, Eileen O, Joan P, John P, Julie P, Suzette P, Ellen R-D, Jean R, Marlene R, Nancy R, Sue R, Susan R, Beth S, Elizabeth S, Grace S, Jami S, Joyce S, Julie S, Leslee S, Mary S, Matt S, Pamela S, Susan S, Cathy T, Louis T, Stephanie U, Anna V, Barb W, Dana W, Kathy W, Joy W.

For those whom I have inevitably and inadvertently overlooked, please forgive me.

Thank you all from the bottom of my heart—I could not have done this without you.

# · Introduction ·

Ten years ago, two events within two short weeks changed my life forever. The first occurred when one of my psychotherapy clients asked if I would form a support group for mothers of adult children. She and her girlfriends spent all of their visits complaining or worrying about their children. They didn't know whether or when to step in or step out. None of them seemed to know how to help their kids or themselves.

Just eleven days after I agreed to start this group, my own then-mid-thirties daughter, normally sweet-spirited and mild-mannered, startled both of us by spontaneously erupting in anger. While I chimed in with unsolicited advice about some situation regarding her son, she shouted that if I didn't stop interfering with her parenting, she wouldn't let me see my grandson anymore.

Stunned and horrified, I stopped dead in my tracks. My daughter had certainly captured my attention, since this boy was the light of my life. We decided to go together to see a therapist, who started walking with me down a path that I never even knew existed. Every day since, I remember with gratitude that I nearly lost my relationship with my beloved grandson before waking up and realizing that, despite my then-twenty-two years of clinical experience, I knew very little about how to be a good mother to my adult children.

And so, nearly simultaneously, I became both the teacher and the student, teaching just what I needed to learn. Along the way, I forgave myself for not knowing what I had no way to know and realized how many mothers besides me needed this information and support. Out of my increased awareness came the decision to write *I Thought I'd Be Done by Now: Hope and Healing for Mothers of Adult Children Searching for Peace.*

As I began to do therapy with mothers of adult children, several truths emerged that helped shape my vision for this book:

1. Mothers struggling with issues related to their adult kids tend to suffer in silence due to two widespread and misconceived cultural myths. **The first fallacy is that our job as parents is done once our children reach the age of eighteen.** When my kids were growing up, I remember looking forward to that seemingly magical number. "Only five more years to go," I would exclaim

to my friends, and they would agree, "Ah, yes, we're in the home stretch now." We believed that, if we parented well, we'd put ourselves right out of our jobs. Looking back, I believe that, when the magic age came and went and our kids weren't on their own and doing great, we felt so ashamed that we pushed our concerns and suffering underground.

In actuality, our job as parents is never complete. Polls show that 59 percent of parents are providing financial support to their children who are no longer in school. 40 percent of adults ages 18 to 30 who aren't students either live at home with their parents, or recently did. Most compelling, 68 percent of parents have at least one grown child with one or more serious issue, including drinking, drugs, illegal activities, or divorce.

2. The second misconception is that **it's our fault if our children aren't fully functioning by the time they graduate from high school.** In fact, few young adults are emotionally, socially and financially stable and responsible by 25, much less 18. Brain research shows that the part of their brains responsible for reason and judgment isn't even fully developed until age 25. I have worked with mothers in their 60s who still despair of ever seeing their "forty-somethings" settle down or remember their birthdays.

3. Mothers of adult children often suffer from anxiety, guilt and shame. **We worry about their problems and about our relationships with them, and we blame ourselves for the problems they have managing their lives.** We feel bad when we compare ourselves to other mothers and come up short. At gatherings, when guests ask us how our kids are doing, we tend to answer superficially and incompletely with "They're doing great!" Most mothers seem to worry about at least one of their grown children, but few share their concerns openly, certain that they are the only anxious ones.

4. **Our society has a double standard for parents.** Those mothers whose children are under 18 are given nearly unlimited support, information and license to complain loudly and frequently about their frustrations, fears, ignorance and exhaustion. But, once those same kids graduate from high school, the rules change. Society's

support seems to dry up. These same mothers must now pretend that their little birds have flown away from the nest, off to live happily ever after. Nothing could be further from the truth.

**Our culture does not support mothers in learning the skills needed to parent their adult children effectively.** This is not healthy. Once we have hope that things can improve and feel comforted by the knowledge that we are not alone, we can then be open to learning how to parent consciously and with intention. Our children become our teachers.

*I Thought I'd Be Done by Now* is a book of short essays that provide guidance and inspiration to help worried mothers of adult children attain peace of mind. Although fathers may benefit from reading this book, I wrote it for mothers because we have tended to be the primary caregivers, as well as the primary worriers. The book includes vignettes, or short stories about adult children between the ages of 25 and 50, since mothers still worry well past 70. Each one wraps up with a quick summarizing lesson.

Parenting has changed drastically in the last fifty years. My mom loved me and offered me many opportunities, but, because she was emotionally distant and authoritarian, I was afraid of her. I was expected to obey the rules such as "Children are to be seen and not heard" and Thumper's precept "If you can't say something nice, don't say anything at all." I wanted to leave as soon as possible. After I went away to college, I never lived at home again.

In reaction to my childhood, I wanted to feel closer to my kids, to have more "real" relationships with them. Many modern mothers value feeling more connected, and that goal makes it harder for us to let our kids go. In addition, kids nowadays often aren't ready to go and show little interest in being on their own.

My parents were typical of their generation in that their main goals were to provide financially and intellectually and to send me to a good college to find a husband to take care of me while I raised their grandchildren. Now, our children's self-esteem and life satisfaction have become important focuses for parents as well. These additions make parenting well much more complex.

**Other factors that play into young adults not being ready or able to take responsibility for their own lives include:**

- They've often been overindulged and overprotected. They simply lack the skills and confidence necessary to be independent.

- The economic situation prohibits them from finding affordable housing with entry-level wages, while graduate school is increasingly considered a necessity.

- Countless available options seem overwhelming, creating many lost souls with either too many or no plans for their future, a condition often resulting in inertia.

- Parents often enjoy having their adult kids at home, where the comforts of home- cooked meals, laundry service, and free or reduced rent prove hard to resist.

- We feel more responsible for their well-being than ever before. If they're not happy, then we can't be. Recent research proves what we already know: that an adult child with problems has a negative impact on a mother's mental health, even if the family's other children are functioning well.

*I Thought I'd Be Done by Now* teaches mothers to develop and exercise the inner resources author Brian Seaward calls "soul muscles," which include curiosity, courage, humor, humility, creativity, forgiveness, persistence, and love. We don't want to let go until they're happy and doing well. Yet, often, that is precisely what we must do, since it is best not only for us, but for them. The book features **183 distinct essays that address the delicate balance between holding on and letting go, a comprehensive index and a bibliography.**

Although each topic may be covered by many essays, each reading stands alone, offering comforting support and gentle direction through a title, narrative with example, and summarizing thought. The format makes it easy for busy, worried mothers to be uplifted through reading one essay each day, or by reading the same one for several days if they find the topic inspiring or challenging to grasp. In addition, the index allows mothers who need guidance in specific areas such as drawing financial boundaries or releasing guilt to use the book as a reference rather than as a daily resource.

**The following major topics and themes are covered throughout the pages of the book:**

- Letting go: the essential task of parenting adult children.

- Building healthy communication patterns.

- Seeing our children as our teachers.

- Allowing our dreams for our children to die.

- Facilitating healthy separation from our adult children.

- Learning to laugh at ourselves.

- Freeing ourselves from worry.

- Discerning when to intervene: crisis versus life situation.

- Forgiving ourselves.

- Detaching from the drama.

- Deciding whether, when, and how to give advice.

- Empowering, rather than enabling our adult children.

- Facing and releasing guilt and fear.

- Learning to listen deeply.

- Developing healthy boundaries and limits.

- Dealing with our children's addictions.

- Facing financial issues - theirs and ours.

- Living our best lives, no matter how our children are doing.

Since parenting well is the hardest job there is, only mothers ready to become students will be drawn to these readings. When we are sincerely open to learning, extraordinary changes can occur. I offer you hope and courage for the journey ahead.

# · 1 ·

## We're Still Their Mothers

What differentiates us mothers of adult children from mothers of young children? One big difference is that we simply don't think we have a forum in which to share our worries and concerns, as we did when our kids were small. We miss the camaraderie that came from being a member of an enormous club which met at playgrounds in the park, Scout meetings, soccer games, band concerts and birthday parties.

Back then, we felt free to ask each other for advice on diaper rash, sibling rivalry, peer pressure, driving lessons and allowances, and to express both our ignorance and insecurities. We laughed and cried and consoled each other, and we knew we weren't in this alone. What has happened to all that support? Apparently, we're not supposed to need it anymore, despite the fact that we think about our children just as often, and sometimes worry more than we used to, because their problems are bigger now.

Today, when we meet up with other moms of young adults, we share vital statistics—ages, graduations, jobs, marriages, grandchildren—and perhaps show off a photograph we carry in our wallets. But it's usually surface stuff, not the real worries that consume us, like our daughter's poor choice in men, our son's chronic alcohol abuse, or how long to let them live with us.

The important thing to understand is that *we're still their mothers!* Nearly every mother worries about something going on with at least one of her adult children. Knowing we're not alone helps us as much today as it did back then. What a relief to discover that we are still part of a vast community in which we can learn to share worries and ask for advice. We don't have to pretend to have it all together. Indeed, it's actually a sign of strength to know when we need support and guidance.

■　■　■

*We mothers of adult children have the same right to share our worries and concerns as do mothers of young children.*

1

# · 2 ·

## Conspiracy of Silence

*T*here is a conspiracy of silence in our culture about the emotional pain often associated with being a mother of adult children. We are not alone. There are countless mothers suffering silently due to strained relationships with their adult kids. We worry about our children's issues, including financial irresponsibility, lack of motivation, poor choice in partners and active addictions. And we feel guilty because we blame ourselves for their shortcomings. There is another way, a path that will lead us out of our suffering.

It is the inhuman expectation of perfection in our society that causes mothers to suffer in silence. We believe that we can avoid censure or pity only if we have raised perfect children with no problems. And so we pretend that our children have made successful and easy transitions into adulthood, that they have achieved exciting careers, financial independence and loving partnerships. For some of us, this may be true. For many others, this is a dream, not reality.

"Thanks for giving me the opportunity to talk about what seemed like such a taboo before," a mother of two young adults still living at home told me. "I think I really felt like I was the only one who fought with her daughter or whose son couldn't hold down a job. I feel like I can breathe deeper now that you've told me how many of us there are worrying in silence."

Now we can breathe a collective sigh of relief, knowing that we are in excellent company: the sisterhood of mothers who have all done the best we could while trudging along the rocky road of parenthood. This is the human experience. We can stop hiding now. We can hold our heads up high and come out into the light.

■  ■  ■

*We are relieved to know that we are not alone, and*
*we will no longer suffer in silence about our adult*
*children or our relationships with them.*

## The Myth of "All Grown Up"

*O*ne of our widespread cultural myths is that our mothering job ends when our children reach adulthood. I well remember being involved in a parenting class when my kids were toddlers. All the mothers there were feeling overwhelmed by constant whining and diaper rash. We reassured each other that, if we could just hang in there for another 16 years or so, our jobs would be complete and we could relax!

What I didn't know then is that parenting never ends; it just evolves. Therefore, in order for me to remain effective, I must constantly re-invent myself as a parent in order to meet my children's ever-changing developmental needs. Prevailing wisdom used to be that development stopped when a child became an adult. Now psychologists know that the stages of growth continue into old age, so that parenting adult children in their 30s requires a different set of skills than parenting adolescents or even young adults in their 20s.

A corollary of the myth that our jobs end when our kids reach the legal adult age of 18 is that they will be fully functioning by this time and no longer need us. Our children also buy into this myth of having it all together and often can't admit they still need our support and, at times, our guidance. This makes our job as mothers even harder. Lastly, because of the lack of societal compassion, we are given little information or support and find ourselves parenting in the dark, certain that we are the only ones feeling dazed and confused.

It is time to shatter the "all grown up" myth! We can shine a light on the challenges that face mothers of adult children and give ourselves permission to keep searching and learning. We can start by admitting that it is sometimes even harder to be an effective parent when our kids are 30 than it was when they were three!

■ ■ ■

*In order to parent effectively, we must evolve right along with our children.*

# · 4 ·

## Our Adult Children as Our Teachers

$A$s I've traveled along the parenting path, I've gained some wisdom from the journey. I've found that parenting often has a steep learning curve, sometimes so steep that I'm exhausted from the sheer effort of climbing it! Even today, my grown children are still challenging me to become a more effective parent. I can improve my parenting by learning to respond to their ever-changing developmental needs, by building bridges instead of walls, and by setting appropriate boundaries.

If I am willing to learn, there is another important way in which my grown kids continue as my teachers: they illuminate my shortcomings. Stepping back to observe my relationship with them is like holding up a big mirror that projects a clear image of what I need to work on. For example, when I found my adult children reluctant to share what was going on in their lives, I realized it was because I hadn't been listening well and had been too quick to burden them with unsolicited advice.

I may fight being a student, believing that, since I'm older and wiser, I should be the one imparting knowledge. But in actuality, viewing myself as the student gives me humility, increases my flexibility, and helps keep me young. To be willing to see my children as teachers is a courageous decision that gives me the opportunity to learn more about myself, to work on healing my own issues, and, along the way, to become the best mother I can be. I thank my children for this priceless gift.

■　■　■

*Seeing our adult children as our teachers*
*allows us to be grateful for the ongoing*
*opportunity to grow and learn.*

# · 5 ·

## Transformation

$M$any mothers despair of ever reducing the strain in their relationships with their adult children. They often feel uncomfortable at the prospect of having contact with their kids because they know that their interactions will be stilted at best, and may deteriorate into anger or icy silence. Young adults tend to find it easier to blame their mothers for the tension than to take responsibility for their part of the strain.

The good news, however, is that it only takes one to transform a relationship. Even if we are the only ones to change, our interactions can become easier, and we can feel at peace. If we have the courage to examine and change our ideas, expectations, communication patterns, even our behavior, we can move closer to having the kind of connection with our kids that we've yearned for. This requires us to become willing to stop trying to change them and to focus instead on what we can change in ourselves. This is easier said than done.

Because no person exists in a vacuum, every word spoken, every action taken, every bit of body language expressed affects our adult children and their perception of us as ally or foe. For example, I have learned that, when my adult child tells me about her problems at work, I know that she is not asking for advice or guidance and usually becomes defensive if I offer any. If I can restrain myself and truly support her by listening carefully and then saying simple things like "Wow, that really sounds tough. How do you think you might handle it?" she rewards me by continuing to talk. This approach is slowly rebuilding her trust that I won't impose my will on her, and, eventually, she may even begin to use me as a sounding board.

■　■　■

*We can transform our strained relationships*
*with our adult children into more peaceful ones*
*if we have the courage to focus only on*
*what we can change in ourselves.*

# · 6 ·

## Pure Love Revisited

We didn't always struggle with our children. If we let our minds drift back to the time when we were first getting to know our new little baby, we remember that we were filled with a love we had never felt before, a feeling often more intense than we felt for our parents or even our partners. As we gazed down into the eyes of our newborn, our hearts melted, and we felt a commitment to love and protect this defenseless little creature. Although we may also have felt terrified and overwhelmed, we were determined to do our best, and indeed we did.

When we bring our attention back to the present moment and consider how we really feel about our children now, we often find that the pure love we felt then has been dampened by years of worry, disappointment and hurt feelings. Although we still love our children, we have to admit that sometimes we just don't like them very much, and we may despair of ever feeling that unburdened love again.

And yet it is possible for mothers of adult children to reclaim that pure love, no matter what our children are struggling with, or how they act toward us. This does not mean that we should allow them to mistreat us or that we must approve of the ways they live their lives. Rather, because love is a decision, we can consciously choose to soften our hearts, to work toward loving them without judgment. We can focus on healing ourselves and the parts of our relationship over which we do have control.

■　■　■

*We can rediscover our pure love for our children*
*by discovering and eliminating the obstacles*
*that keep our hearts protected.*

## · 7 ·

## Grief: Allowing Our Dreams to Die

When our children were born, we had such high hopes for them. We wanted them to experience the best that life had to offer, to embrace adventures and opportunities that we couldn't have dreamed of. Everything seemed possible. Today, many of us find that they have not lived up to our dreams. We may not approve of their lifestyles. They may have embraced values or beliefs that run counter to what we taught them. Or they may have serious problems, such as addictions or financial issues, which cause us to lose sleep from worry.

We ask, "How could this have happened? This is not the path I envisioned." Whether we feel sad, angry, disappointed or worried, we are grieving for what we see as their lost potential. We can take responsibility for this grief and look at it as an opportunity for our own growth. To accomplish this, we must allow our dreams for them to die. We must move toward accepting the way things are, instead of the way we wish they were.

Susan's daughter Jenny had wanted to be a pediatrician for as long as anyone could remember, "from the time she could pronounce the word," her mother always said. Susan was understandably proud when her daughter entered a prestigious pre-med program. Then, during her junior year in college, Jenny fell in love and graduated just two months before her first child was born.

Jenny was so excited about becoming a wife and mother that she didn't seem disappointed about giving up her plans for medical school. Susan, however, was devastated, distraught about the loss of her vision and ashamed of her lack of enthusiasm about becoming a grandmother. Slowly, Susan realized she must accept that this was Jenny's life, not hers. A little wiser today, she has fallen in love with her grandson and hopes to support whatever his dreams may be.

■   ■   ■

*As we allow the dreams we had for our children to die,*
*we can heal ourselves and help them.*

# · 8 ·

## Whose Issue Is It Anyway?

*T*here are three types of issues that interfere with our having optimal relationships with our adult children: ours, theirs, and ones of shared responsibility. It is up to us to determine which one is before us at any given time *and* to learn to attend primarily to our own.

The set of skills needed to accomplish this feat includes observation without judgment, discernment, respectful silence and the ability to admit we're wrong—in short, maturity and wisdom. Learning these skills requires diligence, patience and perseverance on our part, and *nothing* on the part of our adult children. If we want to have the best relationship possible, we must become willing to stretch and grow, whether or not our children do the same.

During a vacation trip with my adult children and their families, my daughter told me that she was annoyed with me because I was complaining so much about small things, such as how old the fresh corn on the cob looked. Before I began taking responsibility for healing my relationship with her, I would have made this disagreement *her* issue by saying things like, "Well, it *is* old, and you should have checked it before you bought it!" Or, "I have a right to express my opinion." Or even, "I'm not the only one around here who complains!"

But this time, I stayed silent while I reflected on the above options, eventually rejecting them all as defensive and beside-the-point. I even had to admit that my daughter was right: *I was complaining* too much instead of enjoying being with my dear family at the beach. I then vowed to cut down on my griping. In a perfect world, I would have also have apologized to my daughter, telling her, "You're right. I'll work on that." But I'm a work in progress, and I'm just looking for progress, not perfection.

■   ■   ■

*We can empower ourselves by learning to discern which issues belong to us and by thoughtfully responding, rather than by automatically reacting.*

# · 9 ·

## The Paradox of Individuation

*W*e expected defiance, rebellion and radical thinking when our children were adolescents. What we didn't realize then was that the journey out of adolescence extends well into adulthood. We can either help or hinder our children's progress along that path. We can help by understanding what they are trying to accomplish, which is individuation, or differentiation, from us. We can hinder their progress by interfering with their life's work of separation.

Paradoxically, the primary developmental task of our adult children is to prove that they don't need us anymore, while, in actuality, they still do. Learning to support them without interfering with their development can be confounding and downright treacherous. Similar to going for a swim in a tropical lagoon with no knowledge that beneath the surface lie alligators looking for lunch, we can innocently offer our adult children a suggestion, only to have them not only reject the advice, but bite our heads off in the process!

It is critical that we understand why this happens, because each time we take this rejection personally and react defensively, we impede their maturation and place a deeper wedge between us. Because they are trying to prove they don't need us anymore, it helps them to know we trust in their ability to take care of themselves. Even offering an opinion about something as benign as what paint colors to use for a re-decorating project can be perceived as criticism.

We need to be able to relay a message of support, or at least neutrality, even when we don't agree with their choices. It can devastate them emotionally to have us illuminate their shortcomings. Attempts on our part to inform or enlighten them are likely to be perceived as proof that we don't believe in them, or even love them. They strike back because their deepest sense of who they are feels attacked.

· ■ ■ ■ ·

*The best way we can help our children become adults*
*is by letting them know that we have every confidence*
*in their ability to take care of themselves.*

# · 10 ·

## Choosing Serenity

We yearn for quality contact with our adult children. We want to share easy conversation, to know their friends, to be invited to do fun activities. Yet, often this does not happen. Instead, many of our interactions are stilted, humorless, even argumentative. We find that we often dread the very contact that we crave, and we suspect that our children may feel the same! How could this have happened? Clearly, the answers to this quandary are not easy to understand, much less change. But if we are committed to taking responsibility for sweeping our own side of the street, chances are we can make a difference.

First, we must be honest with ourselves about what we feel when we interact with our adult kids. There may come a time when they will welcome a more emotionally honest interchange. For now, if we feel annoyed, hurt, worried or even emotionally distant, they will sense our discomfort even if no words are spoken directly about the cause of our feelings. This dis-ease will contribute to the tension that makes it uncomfortable for us to spend time together.

The good news is that, as conscious parents, we can monitor our feelings and prepare a little for our interactions with our children. If we choose to be serene, loving, and non-judgmental when communicating with our adult kids, this will likely improve our relationship. Serenity does not mean that we have to agree with all of their lifestyle choices or condone their values, beliefs or actions. Serenity has much more to do with our own hard-won peace of mind, the quiet calm that accompanies the acceptance of what we can't control.

■ ■ ■

*We are empowered by knowing that, if we prepare to interact with our adult children in a loving and serene manner, this choice will benefit everyone.*

# · 11 ·

## Choosing to Love

Wouldn't it be wonderful if we could just snap our fingers and immediately feel serene and loving? It's obviously not that easy! But what is simple is to make the decision right now to work toward this state of grace. Even though we may be perfectly justified in feeling worried or annoyed, in many cases little will be gained by expressing these feelings directly to our adult children, especially when their situation is a chronic one. We can process our feelings away from our children, with trusted friends or a therapist, or in our journals. We must learn to accept that, no matter what our adult children do or say, our feelings are *our* responsibility, and, when dealing directly with our kids, we can choose to come from love.

Here is a hypothetical situation which illustrates this concept: If every year my son forgets my birthday, and every year I am devastated, I could choose from one of at least three responses going forward. One option would be to continue to let my hurt and angry feelings lead me to build a case against him to include how ungrateful he is, how little I ask of him, and so on. Then I could punish him (and me) through lecturing or giving him the silent treatment.

Another possibility would be to remind him that my birthday is coming a few weeks ahead of time, in the hope that pricking his memory would lead to different results. The third choice would be to recall past years, become aware of my expectations, and anticipate that he's likely to forget my birthday again. Then I could prevent being blindsided again and let the feeling of disappointment wash over and through me when and if my prophecy comes true. I could remind myself that I know he loves me anyway, and let it go without saying a thing.

■　■　■

*Assuming responsibility for our own emotions is the path that will lead us toward the lofty, though attainable, goal of communicating with our adult children in a serene and loving manner.*

# · 12 ·

## Facing the Fear of Facing Ourselves

*M*any mothers of adult children walk around in a state of numbness maintained through excessive use of psychological defenses, alcohol, prescription drugs, food, sleep, spending, or just extreme busyness. It is only natural for us to want to turn away from that which we find painful. It seems counter-intuitive to face something we know will engender uncomfortable feelings. And yet that is precisely the courageous path we who strive to be conscious parents are called upon to take.

When I recently asked a new client how her 30-year-old, chronically unemployed son was able to pay for his car, apartment and food, she told me, "I just don't let myself think about that." We both knew that what she was really saying was, "I know my son is a drug dealer, but I can't face it, so I don't let myself go there in my mind." Mothers like this may write glowing reports about their children in holiday letters, leaving out what engenders guilt and shame. This dishonest and inauthentic approach to life, however, requires a separation from one's true self. It is an act of un-derstandable cowardice.

Those of us who suffer in silence have often compared ourselves to these seemingly blissful mothers and come up short. We wonder what we have done wrong and keep to ourselves our sadness about strained relationships, lost dreams and worries about our children's problems. Rest assured that many moms are hiding the truth because they lack the courage to face it themselves.

To be courageous does not mean to be unafraid. Rather, courage is "the ability to face something that frightens us." It is strength in the face of pain. When we display the courage to face ourselves, we step out of the shadows into the light to find, to our great relief, that we are not alone.

■　■　■

*Having the courage to face painful truths*
*about our adult children is hard work,*
*but becoming honest can set us free.*

# · 13 ·

## Unconditional Love: Impossible Task, Worthy Goal

When my children were born, I experienced the joy of counting fingers and toes and pronouncing them perfect! Wouldn't it be wonderful if I could always have seen them this way? I had good intentions. I vowed to love them unconditionally and help them reach their full potential. I prayed to be kinder and less critical than my mom. I just had no idea how hard this task would be.

My older child, a girl, was an "easy" baby—placid, happy, and able to entertain herself for hours. I remember thinking that maybe I'd have lots of kids, since this parenting thing was such a piece of cake. But, then, along came my son—the white tornado—clearly sent to teach me humility. When he was 18 months old, I remember wishing he were more like his sister. Already a daredevil, infinitely active and curious, he climbed out of his crib and onto the top of the refrigerator before he was two. I ran after him, yelling at him to slow down. I had my first inkling then of what I know fully today: being a good parent really is the toughest job of all.

It took me years to understand that my judgmental response to my son's high-spirited behavior was my issue: triggered, but not caused, by him. Although my life would have been easier if he had been more like his sister, the truth is he was nothing like his sister. It was freeing when I learned to own the fact that my misery was caused not by him, but rather by my intense need for him to be different than he was. It took me years to accept that it was his behavior, not him, that was bad, and it took *me* facing *me* to bring this healing change about.

■ ■ ■

*It is impossible for us mothers to love our children all of the time, but that shouldn't stop us from trying.*

# · 14 ·

## Accepting Differences

*M*y friend Merilee's love for her adult daughter Emma was tested when Emma informed her mom that she had decided to vote for the presidential candidate Merilee had been actively campaigning against. Merilee was so shocked that she burst into tears and shouted "You've got to be kidding!" Emma became defensive, refused to discuss the matter, and later wrote her mom a scathing email informing her that she had been disrespectful and unsupportive and that she would never again discuss politics with her.

Merilee was stunned and baffled by this reaction and pulled away from Emma to lick her wounds. She found herself ruminating about all the things she would like to say to her daughter in her return email. She felt angry, hurt, and disheartened as she wondered how this could have happened. In years past, Merilee would have felt compelled to share all these feelings with her daughter, but this time she was wise enough to know that her distress stemmed from her own grief reaction, and that it was her responsibility to work through her own painful feelings.

Merilee knew she wasn't willing to risk permanent strain in her relationship with Emma for the sake of principle, which she understood was often just false pride hiding under a cloak of righteousness. She tried to see her daughter's decision as an expression of her individuality, not a personal rejection, and she kept her distance while processing her pain. She decided in time not to respond to Emma's email and slowly felt herself coming to terms with both her daughter's decision and the implications of that decision.

Just three weeks later, as she sat down to Thanksgiving dinner at Emma's house, Merilee was at peace and gave sincere thanks aloud for being part of such a loving family. Silently she offered a prayer of gratitude that she had been able to do the hard work needed to maintain their bridge.

■ ■ ■

*When our adult children embrace values different from our own, we can choose not to interpret their beliefs and choices as personal rejection.*

## · 15 ·

## Strength versus Courage

*A*ll of us mothers would agree that, many times, we've been called upon to be strong, often when we're feeling anything but. There is no question that sacrifice is required of and valued in mothers: how many times did we wind up helping them with their homework after a long day's work, when all we really wanted was to put our feet up? Sometimes, we even stayed in an empty marriage until the children were grown. We performed these tasks without complaint, and even with a smile.

Perhaps due to the rugged individualism upon which our country was founded, our society places a  high premium on strength and sacrifice. "Stiff upper lip," we say. "Chin up," suggesting that there is real virtue to be found in suffering. However, we moms want more from our lives today than to feel like martyrs. Cultivating the undervalued trait of courage can take us from surviving to thriving. The following piece illuminates the core differences between strength and courage. Rather than being about toughness, courage is a trait combining integrity with exquisite vulnerability:

- It takes strength to be firm. It takes courage to be gentle.
- It takes strength to stand guard. It takes courage to let your guard down.
- It takes strength to conquer. It takes courage to surrender.
- It takes strength to be certain. It takes courage to have doubt.
- It takes strength to feel a friend's pain. It takes courage to feel your own pain.
- It takes strength to hide feelings. It takes courage to show them.
- It takes strength to endure abuse. It takes courage to stop it.
- It takes strength to stand alone. It takes courage to lean on one another.
- It takes strength to love. It takes courage to be loved.
- It takes strength to survive. It takes courage to live.

■　■　■

*To most mothers, every situation is a blessing or a curse to battle, while, to the enlightened mother, every situation is a challenge to be faced with courage.*

# · 16 ·

## Learning to Laugh at Ourselves

The great actress Ethel Barrymore said, "You grow up the day you have your first real laugh at yourself." This truth can help us mothers take our problems less seriously by learning how to lighten up. Developing the ability to see ourselves as part of a cosmic joke is usually about coming to understand that the world doesn't revolve around us. It is humbling and comforting to accept that we are all inherently flawed. Lasting growth can come through the humor generated by seeing the absurdity in difficult truths about ourselves.

When I feel despondent about some situation in my children's lives, it seems impossible to inject humor into the scenario. But even cultivating the desire to lighten up sometimes helps me do just that. For example, I am learning to recognize the telltale signs of one of my more useless self-torture devices, "Building My Case." Here's how it works: I spend hours thinking up all the reasons why some course of action my children are taking is doomed to failure. I convince myself that only I can save them, and I set about preparing an iron-clad case that would be the envy of any trial attorney.

After careful preparation and several sleepless nights, and before either considering the wisdom of this action or asking their permission, I launch into a passionate delivery of my opening arguments. My poor children then do their part of our dance by rolling their eyes and telling me that I am overreacting, which is usually true. It has taken me years to realize that not even once did either of my children benefit from my carefully-constructed diatribes.

Today, by shining a light on the absurdity of this endeavor, I recognize the early warning signs of "Building My Case" before I do any damage. It's a relief to remember that I am not the Queen of the Universe, just a world-class Drama Queen!

■　■　■

*Knowing how to lighten up and laugh at ourselves is a great gift to us and to our children.*

# · 17 ·

## The Revised Golden Rule

We all aspire to live according to the Golden Rule: "Do unto others as we would have them do unto us." I'm not convinced, however, that this credo always works best with my adult children. The Golden Rule suggests that how I want to be treated should be a guideline for how I treat my children. Certainly, I would like to be treated with dignity, kindness and respect. But what constitutes these attributes for me may be quite different for my children.

Instead, I strive to use my Revised Golden Rule, which states, "Do unto others as they would have us do unto them." For example, I know that emotional honesty and sharing uncomfortable feelings allow me to feel more connected in my close relationships. This approach seems respectful to me. I have learned, however, that my daughter does not share this approach, which she views as rude and disrespectful.

Once, when she announced a decision she had made, I felt shocked and dismayed. When I expressed my feelings, she became defensive and informed me that the topic was closed for discussion. Later, she told me that I should have kept my feelings to myself, that I was being disrespectful to her.

If the situation had been reversed, I would have preferred her to express her feelings openly. But I did not honor my daughter when I treated her as I like to be treated. Although I feel sad that we can't share the emotional intimacy that I prefer, she is an adult and has every right to define her own values and needs. Now that I understand, I can apply my Revised Golden Rule and treat her as she wants to be treated.

■ ■ ■

*Knowing what our adult children need and treating them accordingly allows us to build respectful relationships with them.*

# · 18 ·

## Permission to Throw a Pity Party

*P*arenting consciously has brought many blessings to me and my adult children. These include responding rather than reacting, choosing my battles with care, and letting go when I want to control. I keep these tools packed in a big tool bag, which gets heavier with each new skill I learn. On most days, I'm up for the task of using the restraint, sacrifice and thoughtfulness that represent emotional maturity.

But there are just some days when lugging that bag around seems too darn hard. I'm learning that it's okay to have a bad day from time to time. Free will gives me the ability to decide how I want to behave, and I can change my mind at will. If I tell myself that I must *always* do, say and even think the right thing, I will eventually suffer from depression, resentment or other symptoms of burnout. I can still be a good parent even if I feel angry at my kids for being selfish, unappreciative or irresponsible, especially if I don't share those feelings directly with them.

Sometimes I throw myself a pity party, during which time I complain loudly about all the things I do for my ungrateful children or expound at length about the character flaws I see in them or their partners. It feels cathartic to give myself permission to blow it all out at times. This self-indulgence is even more satisfying when I invite friends to my party. Having trusted friends validate my reality helps me discharge feelings of frustration, sadness or exhaustion. Being careful not to let the party go on too long, I then find that I'm ready to return to the always challenging work of conscious parenting.

■ ■ ■

*Because parenting responsibly is such hard work, it is normal to need a break at times, and it is healthy to ask for support while we let off steam.*

# · 19 ·

## Gentleness: the Antidote to the Shame-Blame Game

When we see our adult children struggling with addictive behaviors, relationship problems or financial matters, it is painful for us, because we love them and don't want to see them suffer. But sometimes the feelings don't stop with sadness and pain; they spread into guilt and shame as we begin to build a clear case of cause and effect. We find ourselves reflecting on our own addictive behaviors when we were raising our kids, how easily and often we were critical of them, or how we didn't teach them money management skills. Gradually, we formulate a clear link between these behaviors and our kids' current struggles, and we repeat a familiar pattern of self-recrimination.

This is the Shame-Blame Game, and it's deadly to our peace of mind. Some of us have amazing staying power and can play this game for days or even weeks, robbing us of leisure and sleep time as we wonder how different our children's lives might be today if only we had gotten our act together when they were small. Perhaps we think this rumination is like paying penance for our sins, except there is no prescribed time limit, and punishment, rather than forgiveness, seems to be the goal in itself. Absolutely no good ever comes from playing this game.

The good news is that there is an antidote for the Shame-Blame Game, and the sooner it is applied, the less damage will be exacted. We can learn to use the healing balm of gentleness to soothe the damage caused by our toxic self-talk. Gentleness is a great gift that allows us to show compassion toward ourselves. It allows that we truly did the best we were capable of at the time. It leads us in the direction of that state of grace called forgiveness.

■  ■  ■

*When we start to blame ourselves for our children's issues, we can, instead, choose compassion, reminding ourselves that we were the best parents we knew how to be with the information available to us at that time.*

# · 20 ·

## Lighten Up!

*T*he very best way to reach the blissful state of detachment with love is to take ourselves lightly, to learn to let go of whatever we believe needs fixing in our adult children, their partners or their children. Sometimes we believe that our world is in imminent danger of coming to a screeching halt without our gifted and brilliant interventions.

Putting things in perspective helps us to remember that whatever is torturing us now really doesn't matter much in the grand scheme of things. If we stand back and look at the situation that is troubling us as though we were watching a movie, we can gain the emotional distance to see what a waste of precious time and energy it is to obsess about whether our grandson cuts his shaggy mane or our son wears knee pads while mountain biking.

Deepak Chopra, MD, the famous Indian-born doctor-turned-guru, while being interviewed by *TIME Magazine*, was asked, "Is it ever unnerving to have so many people following your every word?" He answered, "I *always* tell people not to create an image of me... because, when you create images, sooner or later they're defiled. Be like my children and my wife, who never take me seriously."

■ ■ ■

*Learning to lighten up is a great gift not only to us,*
*but also to our adult children.*

# · 21 ·

## Worrying Is Not Just for Dogs

*I*t's amazing how critically important petty little issues can seem to me at the time they arise. Whenever my adult children tell me something troublesome that's going on in their lives, my immediate tendency is to jump into action, as though they had called the paramedics instead of their mother.

Often they just want to vent or process something that is happening in their lives. But I tend to convert this musing or sharing into an "issue" that calls for me to ride in on my white horse to rescue them from impending disaster. I turn their simple need for me to listen into a full-fledged cry for help, and then I start spewing unsolicited advice. This intrusion results in increased tension as my children understandably become defensive.

When my son shared that he was paying just the interest on a credit card bill, I immediately launched into a lecture in the style of Suze Orman—with fangs—about what a terrible mistake this was, how he might as well be burning his money, and how it will take him twenty years to pay off the bill. Luckily, he interrupted me. "Mom—wait—you didn't let me finish. I've never done this before, and I'm only doing it for this one month." Subdued, I skulked away, tail between my legs.

My tendency is to grab a hold of an issue and worry it like a dog worries a bone. After shaking and mangling and pulverizing it beyond recognition, it's not the issue that disappears, but rather my serenity. Today, I am training myself to breathe deeply and wait awhile before saying anything after my children share with me. Often, after a good night's sleep, the mountain has turned back into the molehill it always was. As I learn to stand back and observe my reaction before stepping in where I haven't been invited, I feel relieved. I'm sure my blood pressure, fingernails and children are similarly grateful.

■ ■ ■

*Chewing on our adult children's juicy issues wears down our composure.*

# · 22 ·

## To Worry Does Not Mean to Love

*H*ow many hours have I spent worrying about my adult kids or grandkids? It seems as though it might be nearly as many hours as I've been a mother! Left unchallenged, I might still believe that worrying is a way to show my love and, therefore, a worthy endeavor.

Instead, I have learned that worrying isn't just a benign waste of time; it's actually a symptom of anxiety that is damaging to me and my children. While it gives me the illusion that I am doing something to help my loved ones, actually I am just setting myself up for another sleepless night. In addition, fretting tells my kids that I don't trust their ability to handle their own lives, a message which erodes their self-esteem.

Perhaps I inherited the worry gene. When I was first learning to be less controlling, my son was a teenager with a lot of problems. My mother was very agitated, always telling me that I had to do something to fix his problems. When I asked her one day what she would do to keep him safe, my mom, a normally reasonable and intelligent woman, paused, then actually suggested that she would lock him in a cage in his room until he matured!

When I confronted her about the destructiveness of her constant worrying, she told me, "Of course I worry—That's what moms are supposed to do, isn't it? I wouldn't know *what* to do if I didn't worry." That's when I began to understand that, in a strange way, worrying helps soothe the terror we feel when there is nothing we can do to fix our loved ones' problems or save them from their choices. That's when I began to learn that detaching with love is a more soothing and productive course of action to follow.

■　■　■

*Worrying temporarily fills the terrifying hole we feel*
*when we have to face our powerlessness over our children,*
*but it never actually helps solve their problems.*

# · 23 ·

## Letting Go Is Not Abandoning

*T*wenty-five years ago, I began attending support group meetings for those affected by chemical dependency. My son, then a troubled young adult, was struggling with substance abuse. I was struggling, too, but with my emotions, because I kept trying to help him, and he was not open to my help. I ruminated, strategized, nagged, scolded and lectured, watching in horror as his behavior careened out of control. He seemed determined to prove that he would not accept help until he was ready.

At the meetings, the members told me that I was over-involved with my son and needed to learn to let go instead of continuing to try to change him. Although I was intrigued by how peaceful they seemed, this concept was so foreign that, deep down, I thought either that these people did not understand the severity of my situation, or that they just did not love their children very much.

I equated helping, even when it wasn't requested, with loving, while I thought letting go meant abandoning my son. Gradually, I began to grasp that letting go, which means to detach with love, is actually a more respectful way of loving. Rather than meaning that I don't care, it suggests, instead, that I understand I can't change or control anyone but myself.

Much to my surprise, as I learned to let go, I became a calmer, more effective and loving parent. In his own time, and partly because of my firm boundaries, my son hit bottom, and I was there to help him pick up the pieces of his shattered life. I'll never forget the precious moment years later, when he was thriving, during a visit to my home. While folding laundry, my son turned to me and said, "Mom, it sure is a good thing you got your act together when you did. If you hadn't, I'd probably be dead by now. Thank you."

■　■　■

*Our children feel most loved and respected*
*when we take care of ourselves and allow them*
*to find their own way.*

# · 24 ·

## My Children Are Not Me

*A*s the mother of infants, I knew what my children needed. I was so tuned into their needs that it almost seemed as though we were one, or that they were just extensions of me. All I had to do was learn to translate their cries and body language into the needed action, and they remained reasonably content. Their needs were simple: to eat, to sleep, to be held, to socialize, or to have clean diapers. It really wasn't rocket science. As they grew, their needs grew, too, but so did their ability to take responsibility for themselves.

Why is it, then, that I still think I know what's best for them even now that they've been adults for a long time? I amaze myself with the multitude of opinions I have about how they should live their lives. They range from the ridiculous, such as what kind of cold medicine they should use, to the sublime, such as how many more cultural opportunities they should be offering their children. There may be some significant issues, but they are few and far between.

It's as though at times I still forget that my children are not extensions of me. They have their own beliefs, interests and priorities, and most of those are different from mine. Thankfully, the logical part of me knows I have no right to issue most of my opinions and my kids have every right to do what they think is best for themselves and their families. My job is to focus on myself and my own cold remedies and cultural experiences. Everyone is happier that way.

■　■　■

*Once our children reach adulthood,*
*they earn the right to decide for themselves*
*how they want to live their lives.*

## Close Your Mouth and Breathe

Why is it so hard for me to keep my mouth shut when it comes to telling my adult children what to do? Did God resign and leave me in charge of the world? What I sometimes tell myself is that I have been alive a lot longer than they have, and I have learned a thing or two during my extra twenty-five years. My kids, therefore, should be thankful to have all this wisdom at their disposal.

But this justification ignores the fundamental truth that the vast majority of my children's issues are none of my business. I feel as though my life's work is to learn this lesson, and I have even asked my children to help me by pointing out when I overstep my bounds. They seem more than happy to oblige. I know I am not alone: Nearly every mother of adult children I speak with shares this issue. Bonnie, a client, even called herself "The Queen of the Leapers," referring to her automatic tendency to leap in to rescue or illuminate her grown kids at every opportunity.

My daughter once simultaneously paid me a big compliment and administered an equally large dose of humility. She said, "Mom, you've actually almost never been wrong with the advice you've given me. You obviously know a lot about a lot of things. But you have to let me make my own decisions and my own mistakes, because that's how I learn. I'll ask you if I want your opinion."

What a profound message: It doesn't matter whether I'm right or wrong when it comes to giving advice. Except in dire circumstances, I must let my children find their own way. I must learn to shut my mouth and breathe instead of stepping in where I haven't been invited.

■ ■ ■

*The author Iyanla VanZant offers an acronym to help us remember not to interfere: KYBYS (or kibitz) stands for Keep Your Big Yap Shut!*

# · 26 ·

## Two Little Magic Words

*M*aking any change in behavior requires monumental effort. It is hard for us to grasp how disrespectful it is to offer advice our adult children haven't requested. It is even harder to recognize our compulsion to enlighten before the words sneak out of our mouths, or to say, "I'm sorry," if we're not quick enough to catch them before they escape.

Mothers tend to offer many rationalizations for giving unsolicited advice, including:

- "It's not a big deal—they know I don't mean anything by it."
- "I have a right to express my opinion—it's a free country."
- "Telling kids what to do—that's just what mothers do."
- "Somebody needs to tell them the truth—no one else will."

A more honest and respectful explanation might be, "I know I shouldn't interfere, but sometimes I just blow it. I can't take the words back, but I try and say 'I'm sorry' if I go too far and hope that helps them understand that I'm human and sometimes just can't help myself."

Thirty-year-old Paula told me about the time when she and her mother went to a buffet-style restaurant. When they took their trays to their table, her mom told her several times to take her plates off her tray. Paula, who had been learning to speak up instead of being compliant and silently seething, said, "Mom, you're treating me like a nine-year-old. Please don't tell me what to do." Mom answered irritably, "Don't take it so personally. I treat everybody like this." Although Paula chose to let her mother win this battle, it was a hollow victory, since they ate their food in stony silence. How healing it could have been for both of them if Paula's mom could just have uttered those two little magic words, "I'm sorry."

■ ■ ■

*While never offering unsolicited advice*
*to our adult children may be an impossible goal,*
*being willing to take responsibility and offer an*
*apology when we slip up isn't.*

# · 27 ·

## Magic Phrases

We are learning that it's usually best not to offer unsolicited advice when our children tell us the stories of their lives. But what, then, are we to say instead? We can provide strong support and help improve our kids' confidence by listening carefully and then offering phrases called "minimal verbal encouragers." These short phrases indicate that we're listening carefully, and also that we trust our children to make their own decisions (even when we don't).

Anne, a wise mom of two, told me about the new way she's learning to connect with her adult children without giving advice. She uses the following three sets of new-found "magic phrases" to maintain the trust she is cultivating with her grown daughters:

1. "*Oh really?*' I say this phrase a lot, hoping it conveys interest without judgment. I hope it says, 'Tell me more.' I hope it says, 'I never thought of that,' rather than, 'I told you so.'"

2. "*Good idea!*' I say this when my daughter shares an insight she believes she's just had even though I know I've attempted to enlighten her about this issue many times. I hope it conveys respect and says, 'You are so wise,' instead of, 'Didn't I already tell you that?'"

3. "*What's next?*' I say this to elicit deeper thinking. I hope it shows interest and says, 'I trust you to work this out.' I hope it says, 'You are a problem solver,' instead of, 'Let me tell you what you should do.'"

"It's amazing how well these phrases are working," Anne told me, adding, "When we're talking or emailing, I can still be thinking all of my crazy thoughts about how I know better than they do about their lives, but they don't have a clue, because mostly all I say to them are these magic words. One of my daughters recently gave me a hug and told me that she feels more comfortable around me than she used to. I'm so glad, but if she only knew…"

■   ■   ■

*We can empower our adult children by using simple phrases such as these to offer support and encouragement.*

# · 28 ·

## Letting Go: A Lifelong Challenge

*I* remember when my son was eighteen months old. He was a confident walker by this time, and his sturdy little legs were constantly in motion. He was having his first experience of himself as separate from me, and he was downright giddy with his ability to partake of life's wonders without my assistance. He was enchanted by everything and was just as delighted with the big box his toy garage came in as he was with his toy garage. He had also discovered the word "No" and practiced it relentlessly.

My little son spent all of his waking hours learning about his new world through touching, jumping, pulling, pushing, tasting, running, chasing and destroying. As he ventured into uncharted territory, he would sometimes glance around to see if I was still there. At times, when he fell or got frustrated because he couldn't figure something out, he would run back for a quick hug or a word of encouragement. I often felt scared but tried not to interfere too much with his first glorious attempts at finding his own way.

This was a challenging time for me as a mom, the first of endless opportunities to learn one of the most enduring lessons of parenthood: letting go of control. Back then, my son was just beginning to define his own identity. I tried to provide a safe environment for him to explore, but I still said "No" too much and often had a hard time hiding my fear. Today, he remains a great explorer, relishing his passions of mountain bike racing and snowboarding. He still seems glad that I'm there for him, but he also knows that I'll take responsibility for my own fears and do my best not to interfere. It helps that we live 1,000 miles apart. Decades later, I'm still scared sometimes, and I still have to remind myself to let go.

■　■　■

*Managing our fear and letting go of control*
*are two of the most enduring lessons*
*for parents of all ages to learn.*

# · 29 ·

## Identity Development: Helping or Hindering

*H*aving grown up with just one sister, I was often baffled and overwhelmed about how to handle my little son. I was clear about one thing: As a pacifist (this *was* the 60's), I vowed to promote non-competitive play and would not allow my child to play with guns or war toys. As he began to develop into his own little person, he was constantly noisy, dirty and in motion. He displayed a huge appetite for adventure. He exhausted and exasperated me, but I remained resolved about the peaceful play.

While still under two, my son picked up a wooden spoon and began running around the house, pointing at us and yelling, "Bang, bang!" He began to beg for a cowboy suit with gun and holster like his neighbor, Davey, had gotten for Christmas. I steadfastly refused to compromise my values, hiding the spoon, redirecting and educating him, but my little soldier was not to be denied, commandeering coat hangers, a dowel from a wall hanging, even the garden hose. For his third birthday, his dad and I finally gave in and bought him a yellow and brown cowboy outfit, complete with gun and holster. He insisted on sleeping in it for months. He never became a violent person.

A case could be made that I sold out, that I let my values be eroded by a two-year-old. I prefer to believe, however, that I matured a little, realizing for the first time that my son was his own person and that, if I tried to make him like me, I would be denying him the opportunity to become himself. I was taking fledgling steps toward helping him with "differentiation of self," which, according to Murray Bowen, the psychologist who founded the concept, is "an individual's ability to function in an autonomous and self-directed manner without being controlled by family members and without emotionally cutting oneself off from these significant relationships." I'm still working on that today.

■ ■ ■

*We can assist our children's move toward wholeness*
*by learning to recognize and support their need to*
*find their own identity.*

# · 30 ·

## When to Intervene

*A*s world-class worriers, it helps us moms if we can learn to distinguish critical circumstances from ongoing life situations. The chronic issues of young adulthood include money woes, relationship issues, car problems, legal concerns, substance abuse, poor time management and general irresponsibility. Our children are likely to resent and reject our attempts to intervene with these issues.

Instead, it's best if we step in only in times of acute upheaval. These situations might include eviction or foreclosure, divorce or parenting issues, loss of employment, clinical depression, DUI arrest, physical abuse or medical emergency. If we do choose to intervene, we can do so calmly and respectfully, giving our children the message that we're offering to help, not to control them. We can also graciously accept their refusal of our help.

My friend Cynthia's son, recently divorced, seemed anxious to get back on the dating scene. Always a devoted dad, he shared custody of his two pre-teenage daughters. But, when he started getting sitters for his girls and going on dates during most of the nights they were with him, they began to pick fights with their dad and each other. At first, Cynthia just listened when her son expressed his frustration with his daughters. He thought they should be more understanding of his need to look for a new partner.

But, after a few months of hearing how their relationships were deteriorating, this mom decided to intervene. After careful preparation, she asked her son if she could share her concerns, and, because he was desperate, he was receptive when she explained that she thought he was asking too much of his girls, that they were still grieving for their intact family and were clearly asking for more time with their dad. After this conversation, her son decided to date only when his kids were with their mom, and he was shocked and delighted to find their relationships improving almost immediately.

■ ■ ■

*Because it's hard on us to see our adult children struggle, it helps to have guidelines in place about whether, when and how to offer assistance.*

# · 31 ·

## The Secret Weapon of Kindness

When I see my adult children struggling with life issues, my tendency is to start playing that old familiar "Shame-Blame Game." The goal of this game is to prove beyond a shadow of a doubt that it's my fault my kids are having trouble. It starts with "If only I had (or hadn't)..." and ends with some variation on "You stupid idiot. See what you've done." After several rounds of this deadly game, I feel demoralized and battered, like a prize fighter caught off guard by a deadly opponent.

I am developing the ability to observe myself without judgment in order to replace my toxic self-talk with gentleness. This Observer part of me watches the drama but does not get drawn into it, and, therefore, is in a position to apply the soothing balm of kind rationality. Here is an example of what my Observer said recently to my Inner Critic:

"I see that you're being really hard on yourself again. I know it's tough to see your kids struggling, but blaming yourself for their issues isn't helpful, and it's time to stop that now. I would like to remind you that you were very young when you were raising your children, and, although you worked very hard, you had to grow up alongside them. It isn't really fair to expect yourself to have known what you had no way of knowing, now, is it?

"Furthermore, don't forget that you weren't their only influence—their genes, gender and birth order, their father, grandparents, teachers and friends all helped shape them. And please remember their strengths, too. They both bless the world in a variety of ways. Isn't it a bit arrogant of you to feel single-handedly responsible for all of their challenges? Please acknowledge that you did the best you were capable of, given the resources available to you back then. Now relax, dear one. Job well done."

■  ■  ■

*Rather than shaming and blaming,*
*we can strive to be kind to ourselves*
*when we see our adult children struggling.*

# · 32 ·

## Detaching from the Drama

*T*he manner in which mothers of adult children approach their roles comes in many varieties. Some mothers yearn to be their kids' confidantes, believing that their children's trust in them will allow them to stay close. Other moms feel overwhelmed and exhausted by that same role, due to the volume and magnitude of their children's problems.

Meg is proud of the trusting relationship she has built with her grown daughter. She is so non-judgmental that her daughter tells her nearly everything. Meg does not always feel blessed by this closeness, however, since her daughter is a crisis-prone young woman with chronic problems ranging from abusive boyfriends to alcohol abuse, eviction, credit card debt and driving violations.

Historically, Meg not only listened to her daughter's woes but felt compelled to rescue her from them, often letting her move back into her home between boyfriends and evictions, often loaning her money and paying for her counseling. Meg felt so guilty and responsible for her daughter's problems that she felt compelled to help her. In time, Meg found her emotional and physical health suffering, since she was always either involved in her daughter's crisis or awaiting the next one. Meg couldn't relax and often felt resentful.

Today, she is learning to detach from the drama. Meg understands that her daughter may always court crisis and that she can be there for her without feeling obligated to bail her out. Now, when her daughter calls with her latest problem, Meg says, "Oh, I'm sorry to hear that, honey," instead of "Oh no, that's terrible! Why don't you come on over so we can talk about this some more?" She hears fewer details about her daughter's problems and is relieved to be moving out of the loop. Her daughter has found another close confidante who has jumped into the rescuer role, and Meg has more time for her crafts projects.

■　■　■

*When our adult children tell us their problems,*
*we can listen and express care without*
*rushing in to rescue them.*

# · 33 ·

## Spitting Out the Bait

*T*here are many ways we can get hooked into being overly involved in our children's lives. If we  learn to recognize what the bait they offer looks like, we can eventually choose to ignore that bait on the hook. Meanwhile, we can spit out the bait before the hook becomes too deeply embedded in our cheeks. Not feeling like good-enough mothers is one of our biggest hooks. When we are embarrassed by our adult kids' behavior, we often feel compelled to get them to shape up so we can feel better about ourselves and not have to risk being judged by others. This course of action seldom has a positive outcome.

My friend Sue has a 35-year-old unmarried son. Like many men, he was notoriously bad at thanking people for birthday or holiday gifts. Historically, her aunt and sister would tell Sue, who lives in a different state from her son, that they hadn't heard from him since sending his presents and wondered if she knew if he'd received them. She would apologize, feeling like a terrible mother for having raised such an ungrateful child, and would then follow up with an angry phone call to her son to berate him for being so inconsiderate. These calls resulted in more arguments than thank-you notes.

Lately, Sue has been learning not to swallow the guilt and shame bait. She reminds herself that this issue is between her son and his family members. Upon hearing from her relatives, now she tells them, "I'm sure he received your gifts. It sure is sweet of you to continue to remember him, given how unlikely he is to acknowledge your kindness." She no longer says anything to her son about these conversations. In the past year, he has begun writing thank-you notes and, even more astonishing, now requires that *his* son do the same.

■ ■ ■

*By separating our problems from our children's,*
*we can refuse to allow their issues to be*
*a reflection on our self-worth.*

## Owning My Disappointment as My Problem

*I* am learning that one of the main triggers for my urge to change and control my adult kids and grandkids is my disappointment about the ways in which they don't match my ideal. A big difference between my daughter and me is that I tend to be perfectionistic, while she is quite easygoing. On my best days, I view this discrepancy as nothing more than a preference. On more challenging days, I place value on this difference and view me as right and my daughter as wrong.

One day, I went to pick up my then-five-year-old granddaughter for a performance at our local puppet theater. She came bounding out excitedly to greet me, with disheveled hair and mismatched clothes, complete with remnants of breakfast still on her shirt. Right there in my car, I waged a fast and furious battle in my mind. I felt disappointed that she had been allowed to get herself ready and critical of my daughter for not overseeing this process.

Then I imagined all the other little girls coming to the theater dressed in their sparkly clean matching outfits, hair pulled into neat ponytails tied with matching bows, and their families judging me as an unfit grandmother. But, thankfully, I recognized what I was doing and remembered that we'd be late if I sent her back in to change her clothes. More importantly, I realized that there would be hurt feelings all around if I intervened. So I took a deep breath, released my disappointment, and off we went. We enjoyed "The Three Little Pigs," but, even more, I was thrilled to see that at least one-third of the other little girls were as disheveled as mine!

· · ·

*When we learn to recognize our idealistic*
*expectations, we can release our disappointment*
*without hurting our loved ones.*

# · 35 ·

## Perfectly Imperfect

*I*'m glad I'm not raising children now, since there is more pressure than ever to perform perfectly in roles of wife, mother and career woman. Today's moms are supposed to have the best dressed, best behaved and most intelligent children, involved in enough activities to position them to get into the very best preschools, and, eventually, colleges. These women feel pressure to maintain perfect bodies, dress in the latest fashions, cook gourmet meals, entertain friends at lavish parties, and be ready to jump into bed with their husbands several times a week. Finally, they feel compelled to take advantage of the progress women have made professionally in the last few decades to advance along their chosen career paths. And they are expected to do all of this with serene smiles on their faces!

Our society is never satisfied, always pushing its members toward perfection. A recent article reported 70 percent of American moms say they find motherhood "incredibly stressful" and 30 percent of moms of young children reportedly suffer from depression. Things don't seem much different for mothers of adult children. Society expects us to have raised perfect children and to have ideal relationships with our kids today. With women's lib in the 1960s and 1970s, we claimed we could do it all, and now there seems to be an accompanying belief that, if we want all of this, we must be able to handle it with grace and with little support.

Perhaps the most important thing I'm learning on my journey is that it's not possible to be perfect in *any* of these roles, much less *all* of them. Those mothers still frantically chasing the American Dream are often tortured souls. Because our society overvalues doing and having it all, and undervalues staying balanced, asking for support and setting limits, it is up to me to turn my back on society's impossible standards and give myself permission to be perfectly imperfect.

■  ■  ■

*If we feel comfortable accepting our limitations*
*and shortcomings, our self-esteem, quality of life and*
*peace of mind will all improve.*

# · 36 ·

## Lower the Drawbridge

We all remember the castle that housed the knights or princesses of our childhood fairytales. This fortress was surrounded by a moat, and the drawbridge was the only entrance to the castle. The residents protected themselves by keeping the drawbridge pulled up, since, otherwise, they were left exposed and open to attack. In our relationships with our adult children, we often feel tender and vulnerable to hurt. When they ignore or defy us, misperceive our intentions or act insensitively, it seems only natural to pull up our drawbridge and retreat. Sometimes we are tempted to cut off contact for days, weeks or even years.

In the rare cases in which mothers are being severely mistreated by their children, it might be best to sever contact. Most of the time, however, this drastic measure is unnecessary. It's only if we have the courage to keep the bridge down and stay connected that we can move past these hurtful episodes. Each time we pull away, we withdraw our love and damage the foundation of our relationship. If we keep the lines of communication open, we just may be able to talk things through.

Kate told me that she felt devastated when her son didn't attend her birthday party, despite having committed to do so. Although he did call with an excuse, she felt embarrassed in front of friends and family. She considered "giving him a dose of his own medicine" by refusing to accept his apology and giving him the cold shoulder. But, when her sister asked whether that approach was likely to help, Kate had to admit it would not. She chose, instead, to express her hurt feelings directly to her son and to allow herself to be comforted by his sincere apology. Then she determined to let those feelings go before they turned into resentments.

■　■　■

*Although it is natural to want to protect ourselves when we feel hurt, it is only by maintaining the interpersonal bridge that our relationships with our children can be strengthened.*

# · 37 ·

## Developing Empathy

*I*t seems counter-intuitive to stay connected with our adult children after they have hurt us. Sometimes, after feeling the searing heat of their painful words, we just want to curl up in a ball and never speak to them again. Moms who tend to express their hurt by cutting themselves off from their children explain their behavior in various ways, including:

- "He needs to learn he can't treat me like that."
- "I have a right to protect myself."
- "It hurts too much to stay connected to her."
- "Why should I always be the one who gets hurt? I'm going to show him what it feels like."

I challenge these mothers to consider how cutting off contact could possible help their children want to stay in touch. When we disconnect, we heap hurt upon hurt, with the end result being less trust and more guilt. With willingness and the proper tools, we can learn to let most things go. We can strive not to take their lack of consideration personally.

The truth is that all relationships hurt sometimes. It can help us to develop empathy for some of the potential reasons for their behavior, which might include any or all of the following: time stress; work, financial, or relationship problems; clinical depression or attention deficit disorder; or just the self-absorption of young adulthood. After all, the frontal cortex of the brain, responsible for good judgment, isn't even fully developed until young people reach the age of 25.

My client Mary told me, "I can't believe what a difference it makes in my state of mind when I am able to give my daughter the benefit of the doubt. I used to be mad at her all the time, and, now I put myself in her shoes, recognize how hard life is for her, and wind up feeling grateful that I don't ever have to be 24 again."

■ ■ ■

*We can take responsibility for our own emotional injuries by tending to our wounds, resisting the urge to strike back, and remembering that life is hard for them, too.*

## · 38 ·

## Keeping Our Eye on the Prize

We may be tempted to punish our adult children when they've been thoughtless or insensitive in word or deed. It would feel good, temporarily at least, to shoot back an unkind retort or to do something we know would hurt them. "I'll show them," we think to ourselves, "Two can play this game."

My friend Maureen was thrilled that her daughter Jan was getting married. Although her relationship with her daughter had been strained for years, Maureen yearned to be a part of the excitement of planning the wedding and waited to be invited to join in; however, Jan rarely included her mom in the preparations, instead asking her maid-of-honor or future mother-in-law to accompany her to shop for her dress or choose the caterer. Maureen was hurt and enraged and seriously considered withdrawing her financial support and not attending the wedding.

Because she was committed to healing the wounds she had helped create in Jan, Maureen decided, instead, to take the high road by sharing her hurt only with her journal, her therapist and a few trusted friends. She also decided to be more pro-active and told her daughter how much she would enjoy being included in some of the festivities. She was delighted when Jan asked her to help plan the menu and choose the flowers.

It's normal to entertain fantasies of retribution when we feel hurt, and it can help to share our feelings with sympathetic adults. But if we disconnect emotionally from our children, our bond will be broken, and then neither of us can feel the love and care we deserve. If we stay focused on the goal of doing all we can to have the best relationship possible, this bigger picture will help us resist the impulse to say or do things we will later regret.

■　■　■

*Although retribution is a primitive response hard-wired into us, we, as conscious parents, can, instead, take responsibility for our own hurt feelings.*

# · 39 ·

## Choose Your Battles Carefully

*I* completely understand how important it is for me to resist the temptation to give unsolicited advice to my adult children. They are seldom interested in my opinion about how they should handle their life situations, and they find my compulsion to advise, illuminate or interrogate at best annoying and intrusive, and, at worst, deeply wounding to their sense of self. If I insist on telling them what to do with their lives when they haven't requested input from me, they become defensive, distant or defiant.

Occasionally, however, there are serious situations in their lives that could benefit from my life experience and hard-won wisdom. Because I don't want to throw the baby out with the bath water, I give myself permission to offer unsolicited advice but limit it to no more than once or twice a year. My daughter has told me that, nearly every time I intervene, I am right about what is going on and what needs to be done. Just because I may see the situation clearly doesn't mean that she will take my advice. She's also told me that the more I butt in, the less likely she is to pay attention. Most of the time she just wants to know that I trust her to figure things out for herself.

This guideline forces me to be picky about when to get involved and intentional about the best way to express my concern. Now I take time to examine my motivation for wanting to intervene, consider all facets of the issue, build a compelling case, and practice my delivery, all before I ever say a word. I know that this may be my only chance to make a difference, and I don't want to blow it.

· ■ ·

*Being selective about what, when and how*
*to offer advice to our adult children*
*both reduces their tendency to feel insulted and*
*increases our chances of being heard.*

# · 40 ·

## Asking Permission to Share Concerns

*I* pay close attention to the stories my children tell me about their lives and try to respond with neutral, encouraging words that tell them that I trust them to handle their own affairs. Infrequently, if I do decide to intervene, I examine my motivation, then determine when, where, and how to present my concerns and offer possible solutions.

When my daughter began talking about enrolling my then four-year-old granddaughter in the kindergarten class that would convene two weeks before she turned five, my first impulse was to scream, "No, you can't do that!" Mercifully, I was able to bite my tongue and hold back until I was calmer. This little one struggled with developmental delays related to being born three months early, and I was certain that she was not ready for kindergarten. I knew I had to do something.

A dear friend, the director of a preschool, supported me in intervening and referred me to a child psychologist who specializes in administering school-readiness evaluations. By the time I did talk with my daughter, I was scared on the inside but serene on the outside. I prepared myself by deciding that I would respect her choice if she declined my invitation. Then I asked if I could share my concerns with her.

When she agreed, I began by telling her that one of my biggest parenting regrets was that I put her brother in kindergarten when he was barely five and still quite immature, because he never really caught up. I then explained my impressions of my granddaughter's developmental delays and concluded by suggesting a readiness evaluation by the psychologist, offering to pay a portion of the fee. I'm happy to report that my precious granddaughter made lots of advances during her extra year in preschool and entered kindergarten in the fall, just before her sixth birthday.

▪ ▪ ▪

*It helps to remember that asking permission first
to share a concern or offer a suggestion feels more
respectful to our adult children than does launching
into advice-giving.*

# · 41 ·

## Expect to Slip

*I* had a relapse in my recovery from bad parenting. I called my son and grandson to wish them a great trip as they prepared to head out the next day on a nine-hour drive to their ski vacation. It began with my innocent question, "When are you leaving?" "After work," my son answered. "I'll drive until about 1 a.m., stop somewhere to sleep, and then head out again so we can be on the slopes before noon."

I know now that I panicked after realizing that my beloved son was planning to work all day and then drive seven hours before sleeping. I was reliving the time he was nearly killed when his truck was hit by a drunk driver running a red light several years ago. Afterward, he was out of work for five months and still has lasting deficits from the traumatic brain injury he suffered during that crash. Since receiving that reminder about the fragility of life, I have been more fearful and somewhat more controlling than before.

My son steadfastly resisted all attempts to talk him into an alternative plan that evening. "How about a nap first?" I suggested, offering also, "How about stopping earlier, or leaving work at lunchtime?" After each increasingly frantic suggestion, he repeated a variation on the theme, "I'll be fine, Mom," and he never even considered any of the alternatives I offered.

After hanging up and then immediately reaching out for support from another mother, I realized how terrified I was. By taking responsibility for my fear, I began to use my tools to release it. The next evening, knowing they were on the road, I called my son's cell phone to explain and apologize. He responded, "That's okay. You were just being a mom." Without my even requesting it, he called me when they arrived at the ski resort and then again when they were safely home. I'm proud of both of us.

■　■　■

***It's healthy not to expect perfection in dealing with
our adult children.***

# · 42 ·

## Writing as a Tool for Releasing

*T*here are endless ways to lighten up when it comes to our worries about our adult children. Taking responsibility for our issues, gaining perspective and finding humor in our reactions all help us have lighter hearts, and writing can be an unburdening tool to help us accomplish these goals. There is actually a release of energy when pen meets paper, especially when we can ignore our internalized tenth-grade English teachers and not worry about grammar, punctuation or spelling.

Even writing poetry can be freeing and fun. Anyone can write an Alpha poem, which uses each letter in the title of the poem as the first letter of a phrase that follows. Here is one mother's Alpha poem, written in just a few minutes:

### MOTHERHOOD

My, oh my, what a challenging job!

Of all the hats I wear, it's still the most important. It's

The gift that keeps me growing.

How will I ever stop tearing my hair out?

Energy-wise, mothering's a marathon. It

Requires that I keep on laughing at myself.

Heart to heart, there's no greater love.

Odds are I'll be learning till I die,

Or maybe it's motherhood that'll kill me!

Despite all this, I simply wouldn't change a thing.

■   ■   ■

*Writing is an empowering tool which we can learn to use to help us lighten up.*

# · 43 ·

## How Attractive Are We?

*I*t is hard for us mothers not to feel personally rejected when our children don't want to see us very often. While our inclination may be to badger them or wallow in self-pity, what we might want to examine, instead, is whether or not we make good company. It is harder, but often more fruitful, to take responsibility for our own deficits instead of becoming defensive or depressed.

Jane is working on not feeling wounded by the fact that her son and his family invite her to their home only for major holidays and birthday celebrations. She moved from another state hoping that they would spend a lot of time together, but, instead, she initiates nearly all contact, and, even then, many of her invitations are declined. When she told her son about her needs and he patiently assured her that he loves her but is just very busy, she continued to feel neglected and invested in the notion that, if he really loved her, he would do what she wanted.

After she entered therapy, Jane began to dig deeper and was able to admit that perhaps they didn't want to spend time with her because she was not very good company. She spent a lot of time waiting for them to call and hadn't developed friends or interests in her new city. She now looks at the infrequency of their get-togethers as a catalyst for her own growth. She has let go of trying to get her son to invite her over and is focused instead on embracing a new, bigger life that makes her more interesting. She volunteers at an animal shelter and has joined a hiking group and a book club. She's finding the depression associated with feeling neglected slowly slipping away as her new friends and hobbies fill up her time.

· · ·

*It frees us when we take responsibility for those traits that may contribute to our children not wanting to spend much time with us.*

43

# · 44 ·

## It's Not about Me

Sometimes I am so attached to being right that I don't let go of my hurt feelings without a fight, but it's a tremendous relief once I finally surrender. The following is an example of how I was able to free myself from the emotional suffering I experienced when my grandson, who lives in another state, didn't write to thank me for gifts I sent him:

After a birthday or holiday, I would wait for a note to arrive and then feel hurt and angry when it didn't. Sometimes, I would self-righteously tell my son that he should make his son write to me. I would secretly entertain the option of not sending my grandson any more presents if he didn't start acknowledging them. Nothing changed, and I continued to suffer.

Finally, I decided to explore why this situation upset me so much. First, I realized I had a core belief, internalized as a child, that, if a gift was not formally acknowledged, it was not appreciated. I admitted then that my son and grandson might not share this belief, or might share it but not have the time or discipline to make writing notes a priority. I could feel the vise grip of my suffering begin to let go of its stranglehold on me.

I also admitted that my gifts were not entirely unconditional. I was trying to buy my grandson's love by keeping up with his other grandma who lives nearby and buys extravagant gifts. When he didn't write to me, this seemed to confirm my worst fear, that she really is more important than I am. But, after remembering that he doesn't write her notes either, I decided that I would no longer let my insecurities torture me. The only valid reason to give gifts is to express love, with no expectation of acknowledgment. I decided to continue to convey this unconditional love to my grandson, no strings attached.

■　■　■

*We can free ourselves from suffering by understanding the underlying issues and by then choosing to let go.*

# · 45 ·

## It Takes Two to Tango

*I* have been reflecting on two questions a friend asked me recently: "Are you and your children close? Would you describe your relationship with them as emotionally intimate?" In order for a relationship to be intimate, both people must be willing to share difficult truths about themselves. I believe that there are four levels of increasing vulnerability:

1. The least emotionally risky sharing is about areas of our lives that challenge us. An example might be, "My boss is such a control freak that he's driving me crazy."

2. Somewhat more perilous is disclosing the ways in which we disagree with each other's opinions or plans, such as, "It scares me when you talk about having another baby, because you seem so stressed out with the two you already have."

3. More risky still is exposing our mistakes, weaknesses, or foibles—the areas in which we feel inadequate, as in, "I feel guilty about your financial troubles, because I wasn't a very good role model and didn't teach you much about managing money when you were a kid."

4. Most vulnerable of all is sharing our hurt feelings and needs when we feel mistreated. It is here that we most risk ridicule or rejection. For example, "I feel hurt when I'm the only one calling. When you're too busy to check in, I feel as though you don't really care about me."

In thinking about how all of this relates to my relationships with my adult children, I do know that we are close enough that we can count on each other when times are tough. Although we have related on all four levels, most of our communication tends to stay on the first two levels. They are most comfortable there, and I must respect their limits. Perhaps I could say that we are close, but not intimate, and I feel grateful for these loving attachments.

■   ■   ■

*If we have more of a desire for emotional intimacy than our adult children, it is wise for us to accept this difference.*

## Mothering: a Largely Thankless Endeavor!

When my children were teenagers, I used to yearn for them to grow up so I could stop being their mother and start being their friend. I envisioned long phone conversations and frequent visits, sharing lovely meals and pleasant evenings playing board games. It seemed only fair that they start giving back to me, since I'd devoted the last twenty years of my life to raising them. Somewhere along the way, I woke up and smelled the coffee!

As my children matured, I began to realize it was my job to let them go, to send them out of the nest for longer periods of time with each passing year, until they rarely came home at all. Their partners and friends, their children and their careers would all take precedence over me. I felt deeply disappointed about this reality for a time. I remarked to a close friend that mothering seemed like a largely thankless endeavor: You put in all this work, and then—Poof!—they're gone. This wise friend, whose children were older, helped me by suggesting with a wry grin, "If you want gratitude, maybe you should get yourself a dog!"

My primary reward from mothering needs to come from seeing my children become kind and responsible adults. It is the natural order for them to move away from me. Although I know they care about me, it is not their job to take care of me. As they have matured, there is greater mutuality, but I know now that it wouldn't be healthy for them to tend more to me than to themselves and their families. I take some small comfort in the knowledge that they will have this same experience when their children are grown. And I have developed the resources to get most of my needs for emotional intimacy and companionship met elsewhere.

■　■　■

*It is reward enough for us as mothers that our children become kind and responsible adults— anything more than that is just gravy.*

# · 47 ·

## What Really Matters

*I* had a good time yesterday. My daughter, granddaughter and I took a day trip to a lake ringed by mountains, a lovely respite from the relentless traffic noise and endless tasks that define our daily lives. We went to see the mountains, green from winter rains, and the sparkling lake, filled to capacity for the first time in years. We fed the ducks, walked among the wildflowers and enjoyed lunch while perched on a patio overlooking the spectacle. I stayed present throughout this little adventure and savored every minute.

On the drive, we chatted pleasantly about family news, current affairs and upcoming vacations. We had the sun-roof open, as the temperature was 75 degrees. It wasn't a perfect day: My granddaughter had a sore throat and was rather cranky; the wildflowers were past their peak; the cafe's food was mediocre at best. It wasn't a life-changing day. There were no deep heart-to-heart conversations, no disclosures of intimate secrets. But we did enjoy each other's company, and we shared a comfortable fun time. For that, I feel a quiet joy and deep sense of gratitude.

This reminds me of an essay by Anna Quindlen, "The Good Enough Mother," I read in a February 2005 issue of Newsweek. In it, she describes asking her grown son about his memories of her as a mother. He tells her, "You sorta freaked out during the college application process, but what I remember most: having a good time." She tells him, "You can engrave that on my headstone right this minute." I only hope and pray that my children might say the same about me.

■  ■  ■

*As we release our old goal of being perfect mothers with perfect children, we can replace that goal with feeling deeply satisfied by having a good time with our kids once in a while.*

# · 48 ·

## Humility: A State of Grace

*O*ne day my daughter asked me a question. Though this may not sound like much, it was an event of such magnitude that I was rendered uncharacteristically speechless. She was telling me about some of her concerns about her son, my oldest grandchild, who had blasted full force into adolescence in the last few months. He preferred friends to family, was increasingly annoyed by his little sister, spoke in monosyllables, and wouldn't do his chores without being nagged.

My daughter had called to tell me about his latest escapades. I actively listened and neutrally responded with comments such as, "Boy, that sounds tough," and "Oh, those teenagers..." After awhile, she said, "I don't know what to do with him," followed quickly by, "Any ideas?"

Because I was used to being neutral during interactions with my daughter, I was so taken aback by her request for advice that I was simply incapable of switching gears and offering any. I stammered and repeated something inane like, "I don't know, sweetie, that really sounds tough," feeling like an idiot for not being able to come up with even one intelligent idea. After we ended our call, 20 suggestions immediately came to mind, and I called her right back and offered her a few of them.

What made this a momentous occasion was not the question, but rather what the question implied. My beloved daughter feels good enough about our relationship that she trusts that I know my place and (usually) won't step in where I haven't been invited. She feels good enough about herself that she knows she can still be a good mother without knowing everything. And isn't that funny? That's the same lesson I've been learning!

■ ■ ■

*True humility is a state of grace,*
*implying that we're at peace with not knowing*
*everything and not being perfect.*

## Guilt: A Mother's Most Dangerous Weapon

*M*others are experts at using guilt to control or manipulate their adult children. Every time we use or imply the words "should" or "shouldn't," we are in danger of damaging our kids either by coercing them to do what we want so they won't feel guilty, or by setting them up to feel horrible if they go against us. Learning to recognize how we un-intentionally harm our children by "shoulding on" them is a vital task for conscious parents.

My client Anne told our Mothers' Group a story that illustrates how this dynamic worked in her life. She and her husband grew up in the Midwest, got degrees in education, and decided to satisfy their mutual wanderlust by moving to Alaska. Anne's parents responded to this news by telling her, "You can't leave us. We'll never see you. How can you do this to us?" Her parents never adjusted to her leaving and always made it clear that she had been disloyal to them. Now, nearly 40 years later, Anne is working to free herself from the heavy cloak of guilt she has been lugging around all this time.

Anne's in-laws, on the other hand, upon hearing about their decision to see the world, told Anne and her husband, "We're really excited for you and happy that you've found a place you love. It will be fun for us to come and visit. And you can send us lots of pictures." Anne was reflecting on these two opposing reactions as her mother-in-law was dying of cancer. "I could really feel my in-laws' love then and now. I'm really going to miss her, because she loved and accepted me just as I am. I'll always keep a special place in my heart reserved just for her."

■　■　■

*Learning guilt-free parenting requires*
*a high level of self-awareness and*
*the willingness to forgo getting our needs met.*

# · 50 ·

## Resigning from the Power Struggle

*R*obin entered therapy for help in dealing with her 20-year-old stepdaughter, Allie, who had been in her life for seven years. Robin's husband, Allie's Dad, was very sad that the two people he loved the most had never gotten along. He asked Robin to see a therapist, since Allie was busy with a job and boyfriend and not interested in participating.

Robin spent a good part of our first two sessions complaining about Allie: "She doesn't respect me. She often doesn't speak to me when she comes into the house. She never shows any interest in me. She doesn't invite me to her apartment, and when she brought some friends over to use the pool, she didn't even introduce me." It would have been easy, though not helpful, for me to commiserate with Robin. "How rude! How ungrateful! What a spoiled brat!" I could have replied. Instead, I listened patiently for awhile and then asked, "Do you greet her when she comes over or show interest in her life?" Robin answered, "She doesn't do those things for me. Why should I do them for her?"

"The answer," I told her, "is that you are the adult. It's your false pride, not Allie, that's keeping you miserable. Allie sounds like a basically good kid, a bit self-centered, which is normal for her age, and hurt by your disdain. Your job as step mom is to bond with Allie, not correct her behavior. You two are locked in a power struggle, with neither side willing to give an inch. But it takes two to tango, and you can choose to resign from the power struggle. If you are willing to treat her respectfully and with genuine interest, no matter what, I believe you can turn this thing around. You will be taking the high road, and you can never get lost if you choose this path."

■  ■  ■

*By becoming willing to treat our adult children well,*
*no matter what, we can free both them and us from*
*the deadly grip of a power struggle.*

## Hope Springs Eternal

*A* wise mom, Suzanne, wrote a piece about her evolution as a mother of two boys, both now adults and functioning poorly. She processed the pain and fear she felt upon learning that her older son had recently dropped out of college for the third time. But she also rejoiced in what she saw as the miracle of detachment: She had been able to hear the news from her son without reacting negatively, thereby not compounding the disappointment that he was already feeling about himself. She was even able to provide comfort and hope for his future.

Suzanne wrote, "I knew my place when my son was tiny: I was the one who had total responsibility for his welfare. Everything was possible. I knew my place when he became a teen: I was the one who provided gentle encouragement and guidance, who waited up till he was safely home. I know my place now that he has become an adult, too. I'm the one who watches and waits and prays. I used to have high hopes for my child. Now I just have hope."

When faced with chronic disappointment, it seems natural in time to give up, to turn the concern into resentment, to turn away from the one who has failed to live up to our expectations. Suzanne is learning it doesn't have to be this way. She knows now that her son's future is in his hands, and he has to live up to his own expectations, not hers.

Knowing that life is hard enough for her dear son without having to contend with his mom's disappointment, Suzanne focuses daily on accepting him just as he is. When we learn to distinguish between hope and expectation, we can always choose hope, which is simply a positive state of mind that at all times accepts possibility.

■  ■  ■

*No matter how dire circumstances may seem,*
*choosing to hope is always an option.*

# · 52 ·

## Too Many Questions

*B*ecoming more conscious about the type and style of our interactions with our adult children is a helpful tool for increasing our comfort level. Most relationships exhibit patterns that, once studied, are largely predictable. One of the patterns I'm working hard to eliminate is the one of me as Interrogator and my children as Hostile Witnesses forced to testify against their wishes. They answer my questions with short responses, often reluctantly or impatiently. The truth is I tend to be far more interested in knowing the details of their lives than they are in having me know them.

It seems that the more questions I ask, the shorter their answers become, which leads me to ask more questions and receive still shorter answers until mutual frustration ensues. I am trying to turn in my Interrogator badge, though I do grab it back from time to time. I have to remind myself that my adult kids have a right to privacy. Things go more smoothly if I don't fire off a battery of questions every time I speak with them.

By keeping my mouth closed most of the time, I am learning to create safety and comfort that invites sharing. I ask just a few thoughtfully considered, open-ended questions, such as, "What's happening with that situation with the disgruntled employee you were telling me about?" If I can be satisfied with the answer, even if it consists of a short "Not much," and if I can wait patiently, I often find they begin to open up far more than if I had continued my questioning barrage. In other words, the more I try to get them to talk, the more they shut down.

■　■　■

*Instead of creating defensiveness by asking too many questions, we can create fertile space for conversation by asking just one or two thoughtful questions and accepting the answers.*

# · 53 ·

## The Compulsion to Illuminate

*O*ne of many relationship dynamics that result in distrust and discomfort occurs when the mom becomes the Illuminator, compulsively hammering away at her children about a course of action she is certain they should take. She maintains her deluge until either her children acquiesce or launch their counterattack. Moms can be amazingly persistent with little or no reinforcement of their behavior.

Recently, I facilitated a session between my client Maria, a bright 30-year-old professional woman, and her mother. Tearfully, Maria apologized to her mom for missing an important family gathering, explaining that she had counted on her new boyfriend to get them home in time from their vacation, but he had gotten hopelessly lost. She told her mom she would make sure she had directions before heading out on another trip. This sharing was emotionally risky for Maria. Before our work together, she would likely have offered neither explanation nor apology.

Without acknowledging her daughter's apology, mom immediately put on her Illuminator cap and launched into telling Maria the many ways in which she could have prevented this fiasco and why she should always use a mapping site before heading anywhere. She also described in detail how embarrassed she was in front of her family. I could see Maria shutting down emotionally, but her mother missed the important signals she was broadcasting and pushed harder, even as her daughter became increasingly defensive. Finally, with Maria's head down and arms crossed, I intervened, bringing the destructive interaction to a close.

I pointed out that this mom had missed the potential for warmth, healing and closure that would have come with her acceptance of Maria's sincere apology. Compassion and a vote of confidence in her daughter's ability to learn from her mistake would have been far better gifts than any nuggets of information she could have offered. The moment was lost forever.

■   ■   ■

*Because offering unsolicited advice creates tension between us and our children, we must learn to bite our tongues so we can stay open to opportunities for healing and intimacy.*

# · 54 ·

## What Did I Do Wrong?

When my children were adolescents, I was a single mom and a professional woman, completely overwhelmed by the many demands on my time. My daughter was an honors student, active in marching band and piano competitions. My son was failing in school and abusing substances. I was worried sick and wracked with guilt. I kept trying desperately to fix my son, who steadfastly insisted on proving to me that only in *his* time would he respond to any attempts to help.

I felt so ashamed about my son that I kept all of my worries to myself. Finally, I cried out to one of the few friends in whom I'd confided, "What did I do wrong? How did I get one good kid and one bad kid?" My friend gave me some sage advice I still treasure: "There are many influences besides you shaping your children. You can only take credit for your daughter if you blame yourself for your son, so why do either?" Her compassion gave me permission to be gentler with myself. I began to release society's black and white thinking that suggested if I was not parenting perfectly, I was parenting badly.

During the 20 years since that conversation, things have only gone from bad to worse as far as society's impossibly high standards for mothers go. I still have to work consciously to remember that I am a good-enough mom. Recently, I read a story about a dad who risked his life and spent a year trying to keep his son out of prison and another about a mom who gave a kidney to her adult daughter. I found myself wondering if I do enough for my kids today. Fortunately, I caught myself and replaced this guilt-driven doubt with the truth that being an ordinary, devoted mother is quite enough.

■ ■ ■

*We can learn to release ourselves
from the insanity of needing to have "perfect" children
in order to prove our worth as mothers.*

# · 55 ·

## Compelled to Control

*T*he issues we find most troubling in our children are likely the ones we most want to control and also need to release. If we dig deeply, we will probably discover that our discontent is caused not only by our worries about them, but also by our desire to reduce our own guilt. This guilt stems from our belief that if we'd been better mothers, our kids wouldn't have these issues.

Rachel regularly questioned her 32-year-old son about the details of his credit card debt and followed up with unsolicited lectures on the evils of debt and a steady stream of newspaper articles, books and sometimes even bail-out money. Her relationship with her son was strained; her health was deteriorating; and she rarely slept through the night.

Rachel began to let go of trying to manage her son's financial problems when I asked her to begin looking beneath what she thought the problem was. This was what she discovered about herself:

"I am worried about my son's fiscal irresponsibility. Underneath this is

Fear that he won't be able to buy a house or attract an independent woman. Under this is

Fear that he'll get so stressed out by having to avoid bill collectors that he'll return to the drug addiction of his teen years. Under this is

Guilt and shame because I didn't teach him how to manage money. I'd feel such tremendous relief if he'd just get his act together."

Once Rachel owned her feelings, she began to realize that her need to control and fix her son's financial problems resulted largely from her own feelings of inadequacy. Because she knew she didn't want him to have to take care of her feelings, too, she learned to keep her feelings to herself and prayed daily to let go of both her son's problems and her guilt.

■　■　■

*When we discover that our own fear and guilt cause us to worry about our children's problems, we can then change the focus to releasing our guilt and forgiving ourselves.*

## More Kind, Less Generous

*O*ne of the most challenging issues facing mothers of adult children today is how much to be involved in our children's financial woes. For many reasons, young adults today have a much harder time becoming financially independent than in generations past. Adult children are moving back home in increasing numbers, and many mothers despair of ever seeing their children able to take care of themselves. Even moms whose kids live on their own often subsidize their children's rent, entertainment, vacations or even grocery expenses.

A wise financial planner, the father of five grown kids all supporting themselves, shared his philosophy—a simple, profound guideline for mothers wanting to help their adult kids become financially independent. He says, "Parents today keep their kids dependent on them when they keep bailing them out. This rescuing does nothing to teach them self-reliance, and, additionally, it depletes the parents' resources, which they need to be saving for their own retirement. Parents seem to give their kids money to reduce their own anxiety."

"My advice to parents is to be more *kind* to, and less *generous* with, their adult children. They can listen sympathetically if their kids share their financial problems with them, and they can even offer suggestions if their kids are open to that. If there is obvious need, and parents do decide to offer money to their children, there should be an understanding that this money is considered a loan, and a notarized contract should be drawn up with stipulated terms."

He goes on to say, "Even if the term is that the child will pay $15 out of every paycheck, that agreement will still teach accountability. If parents allow their adult children to live with them, much planning and preparation should precede this arrangement, again with a written contract, signed by all parties, and including clear guidelines and timelines. Giving adult children money with no strings attached only teaches them that their parents don't believe that they can take care of themselves."

■　■　■

*Being more kind and less generous shows support
and respect to them and to us.*

# · *57* ·

## Paying My Own Way

When I became able to afford it, I began to pay all expenses for myself, my children and their families to go on vacation together every summer. I looked forward all year to us being together for a week at the beach, and, indeed, we always had a lot of fun. My children, as seems to be true for many young adults, seemed to have little disposable income, and I told myself that we would never have this time together if I didn't make it happen.

Two years ago, shortly before our scheduled respite, I was complaining to a friend about my finances, wondering if I'd have to incur credit card debt in order to pay for our week in paradise. My friend lovingly confronted me, "Your kids are in their thirties. They have decent jobs and no major problems. Why do you think you're really still paying for their vacations?" I dug beneath the surface after this challenge and realized that I was still doing this, despite my reservations, because I was afraid they wouldn't make it a priority if I didn't initiate, plan and pay for their trips. I worried that I'd never again get to enjoy all of them at the same time.

After that realization, I took some deep breaths and decided that our upcoming vacation would be my adult children's last free ride. When I told them of my decision, they told me they understood and thanked me for all I'd done. I am relieved and happy to report that last summer we all took a week's trip together. I did initiate and plan most of it, but they paid their own way. I don't know if they paid cash or charged their expenses — I didn't ask. I just know they figured it out.

·  ·  ·

*How empowering it is to know that we can take responsibility for our own financial situations and allow our adult children to do the same.*

# · 58 ·

## Every Word Counts

When my 40-year-old client Steve was laid off from a very unsatisfying job, at first he felt only relief and excitement about the prospect of finding a new position. When I saw Steve shortly after the layoff, he was in good spirits, devoting half of each day to his job search and feeling enthusiastic. When he returned two weeks later, though, he appeared disheartened and discouraged. "What's happened, Steve?" I asked. "You were feeling so optimistic, and now you've got that old hangdog demeanor again." He replied, "I don't know what's going on, but now I'm scared I'll never find a job." I had a hunch about what might be going on.

"How is your mom handling you being out of work?" I asked, and Steve answered without hesitation, "She's a wreck. She emails and calls me every day to see if I have a job yet, and she's coming up with all these theories about why I don't. Yesterday she told me she's so worried, she can't sleep." As Steve heard himself talk, he began to understand. "I didn't even realize it before now, but my mom has made me doubt myself again. She knocks the wind right out of my sails."

Because he can't imagine his mom treating him differently, I modeled for Steve how she could have handled his news. "Wow, honey, you've been unhappy at that job for so long that now you have a great opportunity to find something that's a better match for your skills and values. I know there will be lots of companies looking for a great guy like you. It might take some time to find just the right fit, so take your time. And let me know if there is anything I can do to help." Steve shook his head incredulously. "If my mom ever talked to me like that, I wouldn't be sitting in your office right now."

■ ■ ■

*Even when our children are adults,
we still have the ability either to make their spirits
soar or to crush them.*

## We've Come a Long Way, Baby

*I* have just returned from an eight-day vacation with my two adult children — the first that just the three of us have taken together in over twenty years. What I have to write about is how little I have to write about! As I faced the fact that I was hurtling inevitably toward my 60th birthday, I knew that I wanted to mark this occasion in some special way and invited my kids to join me in visiting the places where I grew up, 3,000 miles away.

I was very excited that they wanted to spend that much time with me, even when I informed them that the invitation did not extend to their significant others or their children. In times past, they would not have been so enthusiastic. It was great fun planning our trip, but, as I told friends about the trip, I was met with comments like, "Well, you'll probably get lots of material for your book," or "Hope you're all still speaking to each other when you get home!" The biggest blessing of all, then, was that everything went very smoothly, and we had a wonderful time.

It was a thrill to be able to share my childhood homes, schools and churches, as well as those of my parents, with my precious children. We visited many of the local points of pride, and I introduced them to the foods and vegetation of the area. Even the weather cooperated. Most importantly, we were considerate and respectful of each other, and we laughed a lot.

I know that they were happy to accompany me largely because of how much I've changed. Occasionally, I noticed traits in them that would have triggered my need for control in years past. But I was (mostly) able to let those issues go and get back to the business of having fun and creating new memories.

■  ■  ■

*It seems nothing short of a miracle when our grown kids enjoy spending time with us.*

# · 60 ·

## A Daughter's Tribute

*O*n her 60th birthday, Susan, a retired teacher, received a tribute from her daughter. Krista's letter illustrates the profound paradox of the mother-daughter relationship: only as a daughter feels at peace with herself can she feel comfortable with how much like her mother she has become. That commendation arrived in the form of this letter:

Dear Mom,

I wish that I could be with you today to celebrate your embarking upon the adventure of your seventh decade. But the reason I am not with you—because I am working to create change here in Central America—is a tribute to you, since you taught me to dream and believe in myself.

Daughters spend a lot of time defining all the ways we will never be like our mothers. When I was thirteen, I knew I would never condemn my future daughter to an unfashionable station in life by refusing her an unlimited budget to buy brand-name clothes. When I was sixteen, I knew that I, unlike you, would always trust my daughter to stay out all night at underage night clubs. Now, at the wise old age of twenty-eight, I can admit I was wrong. In many ways I am becoming my mother, and today that fact makes me proud.

I recognize you in me when I teach language or international politics, since I get excited about passing on skills and understanding. When I find myself reading books, doing photography and dance, swimming, trying new recipes, and searching for time to meditate, I know I have learned from you a passion for tasting everything at the potluck.

Finally, I know I am like you when I go out looking to make things better in the world. When I turn sixty, I, too, want to be learning and growing. I want to take classes and take chances, just like you. In short, I want to keep growing up to be like my Mom.

Happy Birthday, Mom. I love you. Krista.

■   ■   ■

*The more confidence we instill in our children to explore and find their own true path, the less energy they'll invest in being "not us."*

# · 61 ·

## Empowering, Not Enabling

*E*llen often despaired about her four children's financial irresponsibility. She described them as hounded by creditors, unable to buy a house, quitting jobs impulsively, not having savings, coming to her for loans or gifts, and periodically moving back home when their relationships or jobs ended. When I met her, she was agonizing about whether to bail them out—again. She told me, "I feel so torn. Intuitively, I know that I am rescuing them by "loaning" them money I'll never see again. I see how I prevent them from learning to swim. On the other hand, I feel guilty about abandoning them when they appear to be drowning. What should I do?"

A general guideline I offer: Discern whether or not the action is likely to enable or empower the child. Enabling actions have to do with short-term relief that does not lead to greater independence. On the other hand, empowering behaviors provide children the opportunity to develop self-respect by taking responsibility for their own lives. Once we discern the difference, we can genuinely help our children. We do not owe our children financial support once they reach the age of maturity. What they are entitled to is our love, emotional support, belief in them, and perhaps our financial wisdom.

There are exceptions, of course. If they are in college full time or our grandchildren are not getting enough food, if there is a medical or psychiatric emergency, or if they lose their jobs, we may choose to offer assistance. But we must learn to question our true motives for wanting to ease their burden. If we are simply trying to make things easier for them or to assuage our own guilt, then they may be best served by us gently saying, "No." Ellen began to work toward believing that she is a good-enough-mother even if her children are struggling.

■  ■  ■

*Developing guidelines on how to empower,*
*rather than enable, helps us help our adult children*
*become financially independent.*

## You'll See It When You Believe It

*I*t is easy for me to empathize with moms who worry about their adult children's financial messes. I still vividly recall exactly when I told my then-23-year-old son that I would no longer be loaning him money. He had borrowed from me regularly since moving out and had rarely made even an attempt to pay back his loans. I was resentful and had gone to a therapist to learn to be a more effective parent.

This wise therapist asked me a stunning question: "Can you imagine your son being financially responsible?" When I answered "No," she replied, "Well that's as big a problem as his irresponsibility. As long as you treat him as though he'll fail, he'll likely continue to fail. He needs you to believe in him in order to begin to have confidence in himself. And, if you don't believe in him now, then fake it 'till you make it."

She offered this affirmation to help me shift my perception. Many times a day I repeated "I have every confidence in your ability to handle this situation on your own." Gradually, I began to accept these words as true. About two months later, I was driving my son home after a visit when he again asked me for money. This time I was ready and offered him the gift of this affirmation instead of my usual disdainful sigh. He was so stunned that he sat in silence for several minutes.

That day my son realized he was on his own and that I believed in him. That was the moment when he began to grow up. I was able to empower him by providing the encouragement and guidance that helped him move toward self-sufficiency. Now he has a family and work he loves. He owns a home, has a 401K, and hasn't asked me for a dime in twenty years.

■　■　■

*When we express our sincere belief in our children's ability to take care of themselves, we are affirming their capacity to be responsible.*

## Gifts of Empowerment

*O*ne of my friends, a teacher, told me over tea one day about the newest mess her adult daughter had created. "She's left another job, and, like always, she says it's her boss' fault. She couldn't even hang in there long enough to find something else before she quit. I know it's just a matter of time before she'll come knocking on my door to tell me she doesn't have her rent money.

"I feel so guilty, because, if only I hadn't been so absorbed with my career and marital problems, she probably wouldn't be like this. I'm too embarrassed to tell many people, but she's really a mess: she has just as much trouble hanging on to friends and boyfriends as she does to jobs and money. I feel like I've got to be there for her. I keep hoping she'll just grow up, but she seems so stuck. I lie awake nights worrying about her. What should I do?"

When I asked my friend where she thinks her daughter is likely to be in five years, she answered, "Probably in about the same place unless she can catch a man to take care of her. I secretly pray for that to happen." Then I asked her if she would consider paying for counseling for her daughter instead of bailing her out of her financial jam. Therapy would be a gift of empowerment, since a good clinician could help her work toward self-reliance.

I have a standing offer to help pay for therapy for my kids and have found this to be a healthy way for me to heal my guilt and make amends for my shortcomings as a parent. In this way I become a part of the solution, instead of remaining a part of the problem. My friend agreed to make this gift of love to her daughter.

■　■　■

*We can most help our adult children by*
*offering gifts which assist them*
*in becoming more effective and competent.*

# · 64 ·

## Baby Steps

When we moms are learning to empower rather than enable our adult children, we find that it is a gradual journey, one best taken with baby steps. No one can assimilate change quickly, but we can surely make progress if we become mindful, set our intentions, establish small goals and the methods needed to achieve them, and then take the time to absorb the changes before moving on. We can't let go of control cold turkey—it's just too hard.

One of the mothers I work with has developed a new word to describe her gradual change process. She combined the words "empowering" and "enabling" to form the new word "empowerabling," which she defines as "doing less for my grown daughter than ever before and moving in the direction of letting her figure things out for herself."

This mom used the following example of "empowerabling" with her crisis-driven daughter, who always seems to have car problems. "We've bought her three cars since she was sixteen, and she's run them all into the ground. While we did tell her we won't pay for any more cars, we do jump in to fix hers, no matter the cost."

"But recently, when she broke down on the freeway, we decided to do things differently. We assisted her in getting her car running, since we knew she couldn't get to work otherwise and would likely get fired, making it more likely that she'd move back in with us. But her dad was able to barter with a mechanic he knows in exchange for golf lessons, and that reduced the bill from $800 to $90. We're asking her to reimburse us the $90. Someday we'd like to 'just say no' to her—she makes enough money to have a rainy day fund—but we're not quite there yet."

■　■　■

*Understanding that making changes
in the ways we relate to our adult children takes time,
we can be patient as we take the small steps that lead
us in the right direction.*

# · 65 ·

## None of My Business

When I added a new member to my Mothers' Group, I asked the other members to tell our new mom what they were working on. It was a consensus: learning to let go. We determined that all of us feel challenged regularly by our attempts to determine whether or not to intervene in some area of our adult children's lives. We listed just some of the areas that concern us: financial affairs, addictions and problems with children or partners. Perhaps letting go is the universal lesson for parents of adult children.

All of us moms in this group have been working on improving our parenting for some time and have learned that we must be highly selective about intervening with our children, since most attempts are perceived as meddling or controlling. We agree that our top priority remains building and maintaining trusting relationships with our kids. Yet, due to our guilt and fear, we often feel tempted to interfere.

Our goal, then, is to learn not just to let go of controlling our children, but to let go of the need to control them. In this way, we can have peace in our hearts and a more solid relationship with our kids. I heard a great piece of advice on a talk show about mother-daughter relationships. Anne Robinson talked about her book, *Memoir of an Unfit Mother.* She told a meddling mom on the show, "The best advice I can give you is to learn to mind your own business. Ninety-five percent of your daughter's life is none of your business."

■  ■  ■

*Learning to let our children live their lives while we*
*live our own is some of our most important life's work.*

# · 66 ·

## What Not To Do

*O*n an episode of "The Oprah Winfrey Show" featuring mothers with their adult daughters, a 27-year-old named Jenny told Oprah, "My Mom treats me like I'm 12. She's nosey, controlling and judgmental. She constantly checks up on me. She even follows me in her car sometimes. And when I tell her about something that's happened in my life, she never believes me. I just want her to let me live my life."

Jenny's mom Debby responded, "She withholds a lot from me. That's why I'm nosey. I'm her mother — I just want her to listen to me. I follow her because she goes to bars, which I disapprove of. My biggest fear is that she'll come up missing. She makes time for her friends, but not for me, so I feel like I'm not important to her. I want to be her best friend."

Debby's monologue is a primer on how mothers of adult children should not behave. This poor mom got blasted by Oprah, the invited experts and the entire studio audience, which practically booed her off the stage. These women told this mom that she needs her own life, can't be her daughter's best friend, should stop treating Jenny like a teenager, and must give her a chance to miss her mom. Oprah even told Debby that she'd be the mother-in-law from hell! The only compassionate one there seemed to be Jenny.

Debby was totally shocked by this feedback. She really believed that she was just a caring, concerned mother and that she would have the entire panel's support. She had no idea about the evolution that needs to take place within us as our children mature. By the end of the show, her haughtiness had been replaced with humility, and she had begun to transform from a know-it-all teacher to a student receptive to learning.

■　■　■

*It's comforting to know that many moms
don't know all there is to know about how to help our
adult children leave the nest and learn to fly.*

# · 67 ·

## "He's Just Not That into You"

*K*atie came to her session expressing frustration about a situation with her 21-year-old son Matt, who was working full time, living with his girlfriend and attending college. "I call him every day," Katie told me, "but I hardly ever hear back from him. He never answers his phone, so I have to leave a message, and he only calls back every three or four days. I really miss him, and I worry, too. I don't know why he can't just return my calls."

I responded, "He does return your calls, Katie, just not as often as you'd like. The fact is that, just like the famous book written for women pursuing unavailable men, Matt is just not that into you. He has a girlfriend now, and he's busy with work and school. Talking to you is probably the last thing on his mind, but that's the way it's supposed to be."

"Matt loves you and knows you're there for him, so it's nothing personal when he doesn't call you back. It just means that his relationship, his job and his education are higher priorities now than you are. I know it's disappointing that you're nearly off his radar screen after all you've invested in him, but you can be glad, too, because that means he's out living his life now and you've done your job well."

I could see Katie swell with pride as I affirmed her. "Why don't you limit your calls to Matt to once or twice a week?" I suggested. "That might give him an opportunity to miss you, and maybe he'll even surprise you by calling on his own sometimes." Katie tearfully replied, "I guess I should be happy that he's doing so well. It does help to know that not staying in touch is normal. I'll work on weaning myself off of calling him."

■　■　■

*As our children leave home,*
*our relationships with them move way down their list*
*of priorities, which is just as it should be.*

# · 68 ·

## Letting Go of the *Need* for Control

*T*here are three tasks involved in learning to let go of needing to control our adult children's lives. We must search beneath the surface to discover the following:

1. What we're still holding onto and what we need to let go of.
2. How to let go of trying to control our kids.
3. How to let go of the *need* to control them.

With practice, we can learn to monitor what words come out of our mouths and to prevent ourselves from giving unsolicited lectures or advice. If we simply learn to bite our tongues, our relationships with our children will likely improve; however, we'll still wind up with bloody tongues.

It is the third task that is perhaps the most important for us mothers to learn. In order to free ourselves from the *need* to control, we must uncover the reasons we still want them to do things our way. We tell ourselves it's because we love them and want to help, but we can see by their reactions—either ignoring us or becoming defensive—that we're not helping. The deeper reasons are more likely motivated by one of the following unconscious realities:

1. We have an image of who we think they should be, and they disappoint us by not living up to it.
2. We're embarrassed by them and, instead, want them to make us feel proud.
3. We're scared about the choices they're making and want to soothe our worries.

It is our responsibility to learn to manage these feelings of disappointment, embarrassment and fear. We might not want to admit we feel this way, but only by owning and working through our feelings can we let go of the *need* to control our adult children so that we can have peace in our hearts.

■   ■   ■

*Letting go of the need to control our adult children*
*requires us to be honest about our motivations and to*
*take responsibility for our feelings.*

## A Question of Priorities

*J*udy came to her session in a panic, bemoaning that her 28-year-old daughter Barb planned to leave her marriage of two years. She expressed feelings of frustration and disapproval as she described how her daughter had married a man with a teenage son and how Barb and her stepson had been power-struggling ever since. Barb's husband felt trapped in the middle but most often sided with his son.

The family was unwilling to consider counseling, so, months earlier, Judy took it upon herself to become involved. Every day she gave unsolicited advice to her daughter, who always became defensive and sometimes hung up on her mom. Their relationship steadily deteriorated. Judy told me that no one in her family had ever divorced and that she felt a personal sense of failure now that her daughter was "giving up." She said, "I just want to shake some sense into her. How can I get her to listen to me?"

I posed just one question: "Which is more important to you, saving their marriage or saving your relationship with your daughter?" This question took Judy aback, and she answered that she saw both endeavors as equally important. "You really can't have it both ways. You'll have to choose," I explained. "You seem to be power-struggling with your daughter, just as you describe her doing with her stepson.

"For two years, you've been working on her, and she's never been open to any of your advice. And now, when she needs you the most, you're not really there for her because you're so busy promoting your own agenda. You may just have to accept that your daughter isn't mature enough to be a step-mom, but you can still help her a lot if you choose to make strengthening your relationship your primary concern."

■　■　■

*When we strive to keep our connection*
*with our adult children open and strong,*
*everything else has a way of working itself out.*

# · 70 ·

## A Cure for Foot-in-Mouth Disease

*A* small victory in my relationship occurred when my son called today. In the past, I have often said things I later regretted, especially when I've had no time to prepare for whatever landmine he might lay at my feet. This time, the only warning I had that something treacherous lay ahead came when he told me that he had done something big, something he'd never done before. I was able to intercept my foot on its way to my mouth, instead of having to extricate it after it became firmly embedded there. I had just enough time to tell myself to shut my mouth and breathe before he launched into his tale.

Suffice it to say that the story involved making a major purchase in an attempt to bring closure to an important and painful relationship which had recently ended. Even as I heard challenging questions begin to take shape in my mind, I was able to put them aside while I remained present to my son's story.

The question pushing the hardest to pop out of my mouth was how he could possibly afford to purchase this largely impractical item. Thankfully, I refrained from challenging him when I realized that there was no point, since he had already made his decision. In fact, I didn't raise any of the concerns bubbling up for me, because, no matter how sensible these questions might have been, the answers were simply none of my business. I knew he would not consider returning something he was so excited about.

After our conversation ended, I processed this interaction with a friend who reminded me that my son confided in me because he trusted me not to interfere. If I had gone in where I wasn't invited, chances are I wouldn't get to hear about his next great adventure.

■　■　■

***It's a lot less painful to keep my foot out of my mouth
than it is to pull it out after I've lodged it there.***

## Act, Don't React

*J*ane, a member of my Mothers' Group, asked for feedback on how to handle a situation involving her eight-year-old granddaughter. Madison had confided in her grandma about feeling scared when her parents were fighting, which she said was happening a lot. On the one hand, Jane felt honored that Madison trusted her enough to confide in her. She knew she had helped her granddaughter feel safe enough to be honest about everything.

On the other hand, Jane felt torn about what to do with this information. She felt very worried and compelled to help in some way. Yet she knew that her daughter, Madison's mother, was working on individuating from her mom and would likely see any attempt to intervene as interference. Jane brought this quandary to our group, and, as the story unfolded, the other members could hear that Jane was missing an important piece of information that would allow her to know how to proceed.

The group members asked Jane if she knew what Madison's intent was in confiding in her grandma. Did she just want a chance to tell her story and receive the compassion that would inevitably follow, or was she asking for help? The only way to find out would be to have additional conversations with Madison and then determine whether or not further action was warranted. If Jane were to go to her daughter at her granddaughter's request, perhaps her daughter would be less defensive and more receptive. Jane left the group that evening feeling relieved and glad that she hadn't reacted impulsively in a way she'd likely regret.

■ ■ ■

*If in doubt about how to handle a situation with our adult children, it's often wise to err on the side of caution and elicit feedback from trusted others before taking any action.*

## It's Never Too Late for Healing

Unimagined benefits can result when mothers and their adult children find the courage to communicate about difficult issues. During one magical conversation of deep listening and empathy, healing occurred in a previously fractured relationship between a mom and her daughter. On that day, mom tearfully recounted an incident from four years earlier during which she told her daughter about the difficult decision she'd made not to move her mentally ill sister, whom she described as needy, angry and demanding, across the country to live with her.

Although she loved her sister and knew she needed help, her sibling had never been willing to help herself, and this mom's life, with career, marriage, friends and family to tend to, was already too full to take on a new parenting job. Mom then described the deep pain and hurt she felt when her daughter lashed out at her, shouting, "You can't just turn your back on her—she's family, and she needs you," and ending by calling her mother "a terrible sister." Not another word had been spoken about the incident until that day.

Mom explained that her daughter's reaction had felt like rubbing salt in her already gaping wound, since she already felt guilty and was hoping for some comfort and reassurance. Her daughter tearfully responded by apologizing and owning her part, explaining that her outburst had stemmed from her deep yearning for family, since she had little extended family and no siblings. She empathized with her mom about how difficult her aunt could be and told her that she was glad she'd made the decision not to move her. If mom hadn't had the courage to bring this episode up, the healing that took place that day couldn't have occurred. The warmth and tenderness in the room were palpable.

■ ■ ■

*If we have the courage to bring up difficult issues,*
*keep our hearts open and allow ourselves to be*
*vulnerable, wounds can often be healed.*

## Lesson from the Porcupines

Some mothers I know have chosen to sever ties with their adult children because their relationships have been so painful. They describe chronic tension, arguments and disagreements about core values or lifestyle differences as the reasons for their estrangement. Very seldom have they sought professional help or tried open, honest communication before making their decision.

Occasionally, the choice to disengage has been made because their children have threatened violence, stolen property or money, or exhibited other antisocial behaviors often associated with addiction. In that case, perhaps temporary separation is warranted. But, more often, these moms are just tired of feeling wounded and believe it easier to be distant. It may be easier, but it's not necessarily better for mother or adult child. It is natural to want to avoid pain, but there are often ways to reduce the conflict and move toward mutual acceptance so that neither party has to miss out on the potential for love and warmth.

We might learn a lesson from the story of how porcupines adapted in order to become one of our oldest and most enduring species. During the Ice Age, many animals died from the cold. When porcupines started to die, too, at first they banded together so they could offer each other warmth and protection. But it hurt when their spines stuck into each other, so they retreated, then continued dying from the extreme weather.

Eventually, as they neared extinction, they realized in some elemental way that they had to make a choice between disappearing and putting up with each others' spines. They decided to band together and learn to live with the small wounds that such close relationships inflicted. They came to understand that putting up with some pain was a small price to pay for survival, that what mattered most was the warmth they could receive from each other.

■ ■ ■

*Getting professional help, learning to listen better, being more honest and understanding and expecting less are all tools we can use before cutting off our connection with our adult children.*

## "Is-Everything-Okay?"

"*S*he *never* returns my phone calls!" Sandy lamented about her 25-year-old daughter Emily during our session. "Never?" I asked. She answered, "Well, I call her every day, and I only hear back from her once or twice a week. Then we have a good talk, but I worry so much in between. I just wish she'd call more often." Because Sandy was in therapy to work on parenting issues, I suggested she invite Emily to join us for a session.

Previously, this mom and daughter had fought a lot about this issue, with all attempts to address it leading to hurt feelings and no resolution. They both seemed relieved to have someone neutral facilitate their discussion. Emily told her mom, "You worry too much, Mom. I don't have time to call you every day. But even when I do have time, I know the very first words out of your mouth are going to be "Is-everything-okay"? You say it really fast, like that question is all one word, and you sound all panicky, and then I have to spend the first ten minutes reassuring you that I am okay. That wears me out and makes me not want to call you."

To her credit, Sandy did not become defensive during this confrontation, and, instead, took responsibility and expressed appreciation to her daughter for her honesty. This mom knew that she fretted too much and that most of her worries never amounted to anything. She also realized that it was unfair to expect her daughter to manage *her* anxiety. Together, they worked on more appropriate ways for Sandy to begin their calls. Her daughter told her that asking a simple, "Hi, honey. How's everything with you?" would feel caring rather than controlling. At Emily's request, mom also agreed to limit her calls to three times a week. They left my office arm in arm.

■　■　■

*Rather than expecting our adult children to make us feel better, we mothers must learn to process and soothe our own anxious feelings.*

## The Benefits of Being Unplugged

*T*o celebrate our shared decade birthdays, three of my oldest girlfriends and I went on a cruise on the Inside Passage of Alaska. The constant stream of spectacular vistas simply took my breath away. It was also great fun to be pampered by the ship's crew and to share this experience with women I've known since we were freshmen in college. But perhaps the biggest benefit came from being away from phones, newspapers, email and television for nine days. I knew I felt stressed out and depleted before the trip, but, being the trouper that I am, I just kept on keeping on, working right up to the night before departure.

Once our ship sailed, I felt myself relaxing more each day. I was taken aback, then, by the intense visceral experience I had on our fourth day at sea when I glanced up at the television screen in the ship's nightclub to see CNN broadcasting a show about a nationwide search for a missing teen. I glanced away but immediately recognized the heavy, dark feeling in my stomach as the same one I'd had before I left home. The contrast was stunning and the cause simple: When I unplugged upon boarding the ship, my soul thanked me for the break.

I probably take better care of myself than many mothers. I make time for hobbies, cultural events, socializing, and I mostly unplug on Sundays. But, with the intensity of my work, coupled with the people and events I keep up with, nothing takes the place of an extended respite. When I got home from the cruise, I canceled my newspaper subscription, as well as a weekly news magazine I always felt pressured to read. I limited my access to TV news and started reading novels again. I continued to feel lighter, perhaps less informed, but more content.

■　■　■

*Sometimes we just don't know how desperately*
*we need a break until we've had one.*

# · 76 ·

## Hope versus Expectation

*M*argaret carries a heavy burden: She has two college-educated sons in their thirties who are addicted to drugs and alcohol. She has facilitated interventions and helped pay for treatment, provided care for her grandchildren, and had tough, loving talks with her sons. Margaret is filled with despair because nothing has worked. Both men have lost their careers, their homes and their families. This mom is, understandably, struggling with depression. "Every time I think there's a little progress, my hopes get dashed. I give up—it hurts too much to think that things will never get any better."

I have implored Margaret, "Please don't ever give up hope. Miracles really do happen. Hope is what will get you out of bed in the morning and put a smile on your face. You, your sons and their children need to know that you still believe in their potential to choose recovery. Hope is a state of being, a mind-set that tells you all things are possible.

"What you can learn to give up on," I tell her, "are your expectations, your belief that any single effort on your part will propel them into sobriety."

If you are a parent of children living in addiction, the truth is that anything may make all the difference, or nothing may ever reach them. You can work toward accepting things as they are, trusting that your children are on their own journeys, and that it's up to them to climb out of the holes they've dug.

Focus on your own recovery process instead. Recapture your hope. Learn to live in the present and let go of your worries and obsessions about your sons or daughters. Having hope doesn't mean that things will turn out the way you want them to. Rather, it means that you can stay off the roller coaster of your expectations and live your best life. Even in the midst of the storm, you can be at peace.

■ ■ ■

*Hope is a choice to think positively, trusting in the knowledge that, although we can never know what the future will bring, it just might bring something wonderful.*

## The Power of Letting Go

When my children were born, I had high ideals of raising peace-loving individuals, since it was the Vietnam War era and I was determined not to glorify war. I hadn't bargained on my high-energy, testosterone-laden son, who kicked hard in the womb and harder after birth, asking for a toy gun as soon as he could point to one. For years, I refused to give in to his demand for a weapon and, instead, substituted gender-inclusive, non-competitive games which he mostly enjoyed while running around the house with wooden spoons yelling "Pow pow!" Aggression was hard-wired into that boy, and he was relentless in his pursuit to wear me down.

When my little boy was turning four, I learned the first of countless lessons in letting go of control. His dad and I finally succumbed to the pressure and bought him a brown and yellow cowboy outfit, complete with toy gun and holster. He was so thrilled that he refused to take the outfit off, even to sleep, and would only agree to a bath if he could put his dirty cowboy outfit back on after he was clean. One week later, it took both of us to get him to surrender his filthy ensemble, and I had to promise to have it ready when he awoke.

I felt torn that year. Of course, it was fun to see how happy my young son was, but I felt like a weak and unprincipled failure as a parent. Today I see that this experience helped me start my necessary journey toward humility. I accept that my children are simply different from me and have the right to design their lives as they choose. Now a Texan, my adult son's use of weapons is restricted to hunting, and then barbecuing dove in season, but he also has been known to demonstrate at peace rallies.

■　■　■

*It empowers us as mothers of adult children to distinguish what we can control, change or influence from what we need to release.*

## Agreeing to Disagree

*M*y client arrived at her session with a huge grin, reporting great progress in dealing with her adult daughter and her child:

"My little granddaughter Kaylee was six last weekend, and our family celebrated the day before the kids' party. I gave her some books, a puppy purse, a bracelet and a wax string game, but she was clearly more excited about the Barbie's Pet Shop and Barbie's Pegasus her family gave her.

"Kaylee probably has at least ten Barbie dolls with endless outfits and furniture. I despise Barbie and her cultural implications of epitomizing our culture's obsession with youth and appearance. I believe she even promotes eating disorders with her impossibly-thin figure. I had one conversation about my concerns with my daughter a few years ago when Kaylee first showed an interest in the doll. My daughter made it clear that she doesn't think there is anything wrong with Barbie, that all the other little girls play with her, and that the manufacturer has even made her more appropriately proportioned (though I noticed no difference). She made it clear that this topic was closed for discussion, and from then on I bit my tongue at family gatherings.

"The good news is that on this birthday I didn't have to bite my tongue. I even enjoyed Kaylee's elation as she showed me the new additions to her family. I didn't have to fake my peace of mind. I have released my emotional investment in what toys my granddaughter plays with, and I feel free. I feel the relief that comes through the power of letting go."

■　■　■

*Sometimes we can agree to disagree*
*with our adult children, and we can respect them*
*enough to allow them to find their own way.*

## Revealing Our Shadow Side

*I*f asked to describe ourselves, most mothers would use words such as kind, honest and hard-working. Few of us would easily admit to our shadow, or hidden, aspects, which might include descriptors such as manipulative, judgmental and selfish. But the truth is that every human has a dark side—no one is pure love. It is only if we own all parts of ourselves that we can transform suffering into healing.

Joy described to our group a painful dinner she and her husband attended with another couple, old family friends. Joy's adult son Mark was abusing drugs and had just been expelled from college for stealing, while her friends' son was the same age but doing well in college and in life. Joy told us through her tears, "I'm ashamed to admit this, but all through dinner I kept wishing I could be anywhere else but with them. I knew I had to ask how their son was doing, but I really didn't want to know.

"When they kept going on about how much their son loved college, I felt this really intense fire in my belly that I realize came from the shame and jealousy I was feeling. Then I felt ashamed about feeling ashamed, because these are good people, and they deserve my support. When they asked about Mark, I told them just part of the truth and put a positive spin on things that I didn't really feel. I just couldn't face their pity. I'm so glad that I don't have to pretend with you guys. It helps me to know that you love me no matter what, and I'm so grateful that you let me see your shadows, too. Knowing that I'm not the only one who has these awful thoughts feels really good."

■ ■ ■

*When we share our anger, disappointment, jealousy,*
*and other hidden aspects of ourselves with trusted*
*friends, their acceptance helps us accept ourselves, too.*

## Addiction Is an Illness

*J*ane, a teacher and mother of one adult daughter, came for counseling. "I chose you because I've been feeling so bad about myself, and you sounded so understanding. It took me three months to make this appointment." Then, in a soft voice, eyes averted, Jane told me about her daughter's rapid descent into drugs during the last two years. "We were always so close. She was very involved in our church, a good student and a great kid. Her teachers and pastors used her as a role model for the younger kids, and now I don't even know where's she's living. She doesn't work or go to school or church anymore, and I hardly ever see her. I can't sleep. I don't eat. I worry constantly."

When I commented gently about her soft voice and poor eye contact, Jane burst into tears. "I'm so ashamed of her, and I blame myself. I want you to tell me what I did wrong so I can fix it." Instead I told her, "Jane, your daughter is suffering from chemical dependency, a serious disease of the body, mind and spirit. You didn't cause it, and you won't be able to cure it. But you can hold your head up high and learn to cope with it." Then we discussed a treatment plan for this mom: to learn about addiction; to discern what she actually can impact; and to let go of the rest.

Jane breathed deeper, made eye contact, and relaxed. "I've been so sure this is all my fault that I haven't told any friends or co-workers, and just one of my five sisters. I'm so glad to have someone objective to talk to, and I even feel a little hope." Jane thanked me and asked if she could hug me. Mothers still blame themselves for their children's addictions despite all the information available today. There is another way.

■　■　■

*We mothers must not blame ourselves for our children's chemical dependency, since many factors, including genetic predisposition, contribute to its development.*

# · 81 ·

## Privacy versus Dishonesty

*A*mother of two told me how much she dreaded hearing the four little words, "How are your boys?" from family and friends. Her grown sons were both having a lot of trouble becoming fully-functioning adults, with alcohol abuse and inability to hold down jobs just the most obvious issues. This mom felt torn by others' well-intentioned requests for information. On the one hand, she knew that most of the people who asked about her sons genuinely cared, and she yearned for their support and understanding.

On the other hand, she knew that telling the whole truth to some of these people would have its costs, including obsessive worry by her elderly parents and gossip by her co-workers. In addition, she felt a need to protect her sons from the scrutiny and judgment of those who knew them; however, this mom, who valued integrity as an essential quality, felt guilty about deceiving the people who cared enough to inquire about her sons. She saw herself as a liar, an abhorrent label she did not identify as part of her value system. She described herself as feeling stuck between that proverbial rock and a hard place.

As I helped this mom explore this conflict, I shared how to distinguish privacy from dishonesty. When someone chooses to lie, she consciously misleads others for personal gain. On the other hand, when a person chooses to keep information private, she has no plan to deceive. Rather, this withholding of the truth generally benefits everyone and harms no one.

As this devoted mom came to understand how this distinction applied to her situation, she felt relieved, reflecting that she would now feel more comfortable determining the appropriate level of sharing for each of her relationships. She could see how neither her frail parents nor most of her co-workers would benefit from knowing the details of her sons' lives.

### ·  ·  ·

*When it comes to telling others about the problems of our adult children, choosing to keep some information private indicates discretion rather than lying.*

# · 82 ·

## Should: the Six-Letter, Sixty-Ton Dragon

Some days the heavy burden of the guilt I feel about my adult children's struggles threatens to suffocate me. I go over and over in my head what their issues are, and then I beat myself up about how I contributed to, or even caused, these problems: I was too involved in my own career. I didn't spend enough quality time with them. I didn't persevere to find them the right kind of help. I didn't encourage them to bring friends home enough, and so on.

Underlying all of these regrets are the toxic words "should" and "shouldn't," as in: I shouldn't have been so involved in my career. I should have spent more quality time with them. I should have encouraged them to bring home their friends, and so on. This critical self-talk is not only unproductive, it also damages self-esteem. The underlying message is: "I am not a good-enough mother, and it is my fault that my children have problems today."

I have learned many things that would allow me to be a more enlightened and effective parent if I were raising kids today. But hindsight, as they say, is always 20-20. It is simply not fair to flog myself for not knowing things I had no way to know back then.

Whenever I find myself ruminating about my role in my children's issues, I try and recognize the Should Dragon has been aroused from its slumber and has raised its ugly head. I can either practice thought-stopping or healthy distraction until the Dragon falls asleep again, or I can work on healing the underlying shame by affirming that I did the best I could with the information available to me at the time. I truly was the best mother I knew how to be.

■   ■   ■

*The words "should" and "shouldn't"*
*can be damaging to our identity as mothers and,*
*as such, "should" be used sparingly.*

# · 83 ·

## Getting It

Jan has come a long way in her journey toward healing her relationship with her grown daughter. When Amanda had the courage to confront her mom lovingly with examples of how controlling and judgmental she could be, Jan was arrogant and self-righteous and would respond defiantly. "That's just who I am. I'm that way with everybody. Don't take it so personally."

Through time, Jan has been learning to listen to her daughter's concerns and to take responsibility for her critical, controlling communication style. She used to believe that she had the right to tell Amanda what to do and to say anything she felt like saying, no matter how angry or hurt her daughter might be as a result. She explained, "I wanted an 'Amanda-Perfect-in-Every-Way' doll. Her being so human just didn't fit my image of how she should be, and the discrepancy would leave me judgmental and crabby. No wonder she avoided me; I would have avoided me, too. I made us both miserable, and I rarely enjoyed her company."

Jan described the internal shift that has taken place as a result of her hard work: "I get it now. I've been forced to evolve in my role as parent in order to move in the direction of having the relationship with Amanda that I've always wanted. I have had to eat a lot of humble pie to finally get that I was creating my own (and her) misery, and that pie stuck in my throat for a long time. I realize now that she's not my little doll, and I have no right to try and form her in my image. She's her own person now, and I'm learning to appreciate her for the wonderful, bright, capable woman she is. I'm really proud to be her mom."

■ ■ ■

*Although it's hard to admit our own emotional immaturity, becoming humble may lead to the relationship we've always dreamed of.*

## Letting Go — a Visceral Experience

*L*earning to let go is a critical parenting skill that we begin to learn when our children are toddlers, first venturing out to explore their exciting new world. We may recall the tight, clenched feeling we felt in our stomachs as they toddled around the furniture, often wobbly and uncertain. We imagined them cracking their heads or their chins open and being rushed to the hospital.

This actually did happen to my son, the intrepid explorer, three times before he started kindergarten. Three trips to the emergency room and three sets of stitches only solidified my instinct to try and prevent more hurt. "Be careful!" I often implored while reaching out with involuntary jerks of protection.

That tense feeling in my stomach — fear — made me face the reality that I couldn't stop him from hurting himself. I knew I had to let go, and I was terrified. If I had understood then that he had to fall in order to learn to walk and run, I might have found it easier to release the fear. I had no idea then how much easier it was to let go when he was little than it would be when he got older. I guess we need our children's entire childhood to practice.

Our tendency to hold on is a big impediment to our children's growth and individuation, and it holds us back, too. We may be holding onto:

- Our need to feel responsible for their success or happiness.
- The compulsion to fix their problems.
- The need to be right or in control.
- Our dreams for their future.

Beneath the need to hold on is that old fear, that tight feeling in our stomachs. We can give ourselves the blessed relief that comes from letting go when we begin to recognize the difference between what we can and what we cannot change.

■　■　■

*We can release the tension in our stomachs by exploring what we're holding onto and when it is time to let go.*

# · 85 ·

## The Pros and Cons of Worrying

*M*any mid-life mothers seem to spend much of their free time worrying. It's as though we believe if our kids are suffering, we must suffer. Once we begin to grasp the truth that worrying is destructive, rather than productive, we can begin to use tools to stop worrying and start enjoying our lives.

A complicating factor, however, is that many mothers believe that worrying serves some useful purpose, even though it actually destroys our peace of mind. Worrying can give us the illusion that we are doing something to help our children. It can allow us to believe that we are more connected to them than we actually are. And because it is so consuming, it can even prevent us from feeling guilt and fear.

When my son was struggling as a young adult, my mom used to lie awake at night worrying about him and then call me to demand that I do something to help him. Having done everything recommended to me by professionals, I was learning to let go, and I suggested to my mother that she might want to work on not worrying so much. She answered incredulously, "What are you talking about? I wouldn't know what to do with myself if I wasn't worrying." Since then, I have spoken with many mothers who believe that worrying about their adult children is one of the best ways to demonstrate their love.

In actuality, even if our children are struggling, there are far more effective ways to convey our love than through worrying. We can express our confidence in them and acknowledge their gifts and strengths. We can show interest in their lives and spend quality time with them. We can listen to them and be there if they ask for our help. And, perhaps most importantly, we can keep our own lives as full and enjoyable as possible so they can see that we are not burdened by worrying about them.

■　■　■

*Worrying about our adult children is a destructive,*
*rather than a life-affirming activity.*

# · 86 ·

## Play Equals Freedom from Worry

*I*n order to make it worth our while to worry less, we must develop other activities to fill the time we used to spend worrying. As we learn to let go of our adult children, we mothers, already hard workers, often simply substitute more work or find someone else to worry about. But these endeavors may not feed our starving souls. On the other hand, if we entice our own inner child to come out and play, this invitation will likely result in more laughing and less worrying.

When I was raising my children, I rarely took time to play. I was always "too busy" to sit on the floor and create Lego buildings or puppet shows. I didn't understand the value of cultivating fun, believing, instead, that I constantly had to prove my inherent worth by being productive. Many years later, as I gradually became aware of how quickly time was passing, I began taking piano lessons for the first time in forty years, just for the sheer joy of being able to master a piece. I also developed a passion for creating memory books for family and friends, and my soul is fed by attending plays, concerts or festivals nearly every weekend. Maybe my most fruitful resource has been my grandchildren, eager to teach me to play.

Other mothers I know play by writing poetry, sewing doll clothes for their grandchildren, hiking, making jewelry or taking tap dance lessons. Many find clues to fulfilling play as adults in their childhood interests. While involved in play, they become fully engaged in the present moment and stop worrying about their children, or anything else for that matter. Play is natural exhilaration, not addictive escape, such as shopping for things we don't need or mindlessly overeating. The sole purpose of play is enjoyment, and life is meant to be enjoyed.

■ ■ ■

*It's never too late to have a happy childhood.*

## Energy Drains

*O*ne of the benefits of learning to live consciously is that we can use our newfound awareness to gauge how it *feels* to be with our children. Although we may want to believe that we'd rather spend time with them than other people, some of us admit that spending time together is more fun in our imaginations than it is in reality. The sad truth is that some people, including our children or their partners, exude negative energy that leaves us feeling exhausted and depressed.

When we consider those people we enjoy most, we identify ones who are open-hearted and happy to see us. Because they exude positive energy, we feel better just being around them and are energized by our visits. On the other hand, we feel tense or guarded around people who exude negative energy, and our energy is depleted by spending time with them.

Rose reluctantly admitted that, even when she was in a great mood at the beginning of a visit with her daughter and her family, she nearly always felt exhausted, dejected and even physically ill by the time she left. She lamented, "I feel so guilty saying this out loud. I think I should love being with them, and, instead, I can't wait to leave."

I encouraged Rose to trust her perception and to explore the cause of the negative energy that depleted her. Intuitively, she began to realize that the negative "vibes" came from her son-in-law, who tended to be a sullen and self-centered man. After this realization, Rose limited her time with him and planned more outings with just her daughter and grandchildren. She was amazed by how much more positive and happy she felt. Even though she had been concerned that her daughter would pick up on the changes and challenge her mom, no one ever said a word. It occurred to Rose that maybe everyone was better off with this new arrangement.

■ ■ ■

*While painful, admitting that it's not always enjoyable to spend time with our adult children or their partners gives us more options for better self-care.*

# · 88 ·

## Our Children's Partners

*M*any mid-life mothers are disappointed by their children's choice of partners. Because we want them to be happy, we hope that they will choose life partners who are emotionally mature, kind, hard-working, intelligent and have good morals and values. In actuality, choosing a partner is a complex, largely unconscious process over which we have little or no control, and their choices often bare little resemblance to what we hoped for.

It's especially hard when we see our children heading straight onto what we are certain is a path of destruction, knowing that we can't save them. Rarely do our adult children consult us before choosing their mates—they only want our blessing. If we balk at their choices, chances are they will still move forward without the blessing.

A friend shared that her daughter, having recently survived a difficult break-up from a five-year relationship fueled by alcohol and financial problems, had a new boyfriend. My friend became anxious as her daughter began dating again. "I see all kinds of red flags: He's always late. He dropped out of college and is still trying to 'find himself.' Even though he's an improvement over the last one, I just wanted her to be really picky this time, and she didn't wait very long."

Then this wise mom heard her own words and said, "I know that if I say anything, it will push her even deeper into his arms. I guess I'm still just that mom on the playground watching, terrified, as she goes down the slide for the first time. It's all I can do to keep from rushing in to protect her. The stakes are higher now, but the lesson is the same: I've just got to let go and give her the chance to find her own way and make her own mistakes. Then maybe she'll let me be there for her if she falls down again."

■ ■ ■

*An important and difficult parental task is to respect*
*our children enough to allow them to make their own*
*choices of partner without our interference.*

# · 89 ·

## Happy Holidays

*E*very year mothers worry about their adult children and the holidays. Concerns include:

- I spend so much more time with them than usual during the holidays, and I'm not sure they enjoy it any more than I do.
- It breaks my heart, but I don't know if I can invite her for Thanksgiving, since she got so drunk last year.
- They seem more interested in what I'm getting the grandchildren than in me--It's like I'm an ATM machine.
- I just keep thinking how it's supposed to be this time of year—Families sitting around the fireplace, laughing—and I wonder what happened to us.
- I work so hard trying to make everything nice for them that I usually wind up getting sick.

At holiday time, expectations of peak experiences are so high that we are all nearly destined for disappointment. We can take responsibility for our own happiness by getting the focus off of our children and onto our own needs. Asking these questions may enable us to create pleasant memories:

- What do I need to make this a more successful, meaningful holiday?
- What requests for changes in behavior might I like to make of my family this year?
- What limits or boundaries do I need to set for myself or my children?
- What dreams might it help for me to let go of?

One mom decided to set a much lower spending limit on presents for her grandkids, involving them in choosing one or two things they would most cherish. Another chose not to allow alcohol at Thanksgiving dinner, even if that meant her daughter might not attend. A third, dreading another chaotic family gathering, traveled out of state to spend time with dear friends who had been inviting her to visit for years.

■　■　■

*Taking responsibility for our own happiness at holiday time allows us to create joy and meaning and keeps us from feeling like victims.*

# · 90 ·

## The Paralysis of Analysis

*I*t is natural to want to understand why our children are struggling. We spend countless hours trying to make sense of things that seem senseless. We seem to believe that if we can just figure out why they're having the troubles they're having we can then fix their problems.

The mother of a young man addicted to drugs told me tearfully during our initial session, "I've spent the whole last year trying to figure out what went wrong. I certainly didn't raise my son to be a drug addict, that's for sure. He's not stupid, and he used to say he was never even going to try drugs. Maybe it has to do with his dad and me divorcing when he was seven. Or maybe it's because he was so short until he was fifteen. I lie awake asking 'Why?' over and over again. I've just got to get some answers."

After listening to her anguished lament, I told this mom gently, "I think you might be asking the wrong question. A far better question might be, 'What can I do to help my son and myself?' There are no doubt many factors—some genetic, some situational, some social and some psychological—that contributed to the development of this addiction, but even a clear understanding of all those elements won't change anything."

If this parent sounds like you, asking, "What can I do?" takes you out of the analytic trap and into positive action. I told this mother that there are always things she can do to help herself and maybe even her son. Trying to figure it all out immobilizes, while action promotes momentum, growth and hope. It's more effective to look at what you have and haven't done and then develop a plan of action, becoming a part of the solution instead of being a part of the problem.

■ ■ ■

*Analyzing why our adult children are suffering is a dead-end street that leads only to blame and regret, whereas asking, "What can I do?" keeps us grounded in practicality and hope.*

## Catch Them Doing Something Right

*I*n the United States, the land of opportunity, it's considered a virtue never to be satisfied with what we have. It's a blessing to live in a country where so many have the chance to achieve so much; however, this insatiable hunger for more often leaves us in a state of agitation, driven by dreams of what we don't have.

Even our view of our adult children is often infused with this belief that they're never quite good enough. Our criticisms often outweigh our appreciations. Our proverbial cup tends to be half empty, rather than half full. And yet it is our kids' anticipation of criticism or correction that accounts for much of the tension between us. The most benefit will stem from us learning to compliment them authentically, which will give them the gift of love straight from our hearts.

Joanne described her visits with her adult children as "somewhat unsatisfying." She said, "I am always excited to see them, but when they're with me I seem to spend too much time making critical comments about things in their lives, from what kind of toothpaste they use to what movies they've seen. They're both actually doing quite well, but, instead of expressing appreciation, it's like it's never enough for me. Even I can tell that I'm being obnoxious, and I think this bad habit makes them not want to hang out with me very often. The other day, my son Andy, normally a low-keyed, good-natured kid, got exasperated and asked, 'Can't you ever be satisfied with anything I do, Mom?' It hurt me, but I knew he was right."

The truth is that everyone has doubts and insecurities, and it always feels good to be acknowledged. If we take the time to express what we treasure and admire about our adult children, they will want to spend time with us, too.

■ ■ ■

*Although it may seem unnatural at first, it is well worth the effort to catch our children doing something right.*

# · 92 ·

## Never Give Up Hope

*L*ea, the mom of a 40-year-old chemically dependent son, arrived for her counseling appointment with a big smile on her face. "You were right. You should never give up hope that things can get better." She then told me how her son, a drug addict with a degree in engineering, had recently entered inpatient treatment. Lea exulted through her tears, "I was the only one in the world who hadn't given up on him: He'd lost his family, his career, his home and the respect of everyone who knew him. But I waited, hoping that he'd finally hit bottom, ready to use that moment to help him help himself. Because of my boundaries and my patience, I'm finally getting my son back!"

She continued, "Sure enough, he came to me again, desperate because he'd had to pawn his truck to pay his rent and then didn't have the money to save his truck from being sold by the pawnshop. He begged me to help him. 'That truck is all I've got left in the world, Mom. Please help me.' Time stood still for me, and I just knew this was the moment I'd been praying for. I told him, 'Son, if you go into treatment right now, I'll save your truck, and, if you complete your program, embrace a sober lifestyle and get a job, I'll let you buy your truck back from me.' He agreed immediately.

"Now, three weeks later, I see light in his eyes again. He's talking about wanting to see his daughters for the first time in years. If I had lost hope and turned my back on him like everyone else, he would never have had this opportunity for a new life. No matter what happens, I know I will always be grateful that I could give him this chance to help himself. I had to love him more than he could love himself."

■　■　■

*Maintaining hope that things will improve, even in the face of overwhelming odds, is an essential tool for mothers of adult children.*

# · 93 ·

## Expressing Hurt Feelings

*B*ecause we tend to be more sensitive to what our kids say and do than we are to others, sometimes we get our feelings hurt by our adult children. Then we tend to respond either by blowing up or by keeping our feelings bottled up. When used judiciously, a third option is to deal with the issue directly in a manner which discourages defensiveness and encourages resolution.

After a lifetime of bottling up hurt feelings, Ruth wanted to explore this third choice. When she described a year-long pattern of thoughtlessness and insensitivity on the part of her son, I asked her to work on a letter to her son in which she would share her feelings, give examples and ask for specific changes in behavior. She wrote many versions and, when she was finally ready to confront her son, she sent her letter off. Included were "I" statements of positive intention such as "If I didn't love you and believe we could work this through, I wouldn't be writing to you."

We anticipated her son's likely responses, including the worstcase scenarios of raging or ignoring her, and we rehearsed the phone call Ruth would make to follow up. Although she felt nervous, she also felt empowered and hopeful. When she came to her next appointment, she was beaming. "That was amazing. He called me right after he got the letter and took responsibility for everything, admitting that he could understand why I've felt hurt and then apologizing. He said he's been under so much pressure at work that he has taken his stress out on the people he loves the most. I couldn't have asked for a better response—my heart is full. No more holding in hurt feelings for me!"

■  ■  ■

*Sometimes our adult children hurt us without*
*realizing it, and expressing our feelings in a direct*
*and kind manner can often lead to a positive outcome.*

## You Just Never Know

This is the first entry I've written in the last six weeks because my beloved daughter became gravely ill, and writing has been the last thing on my mind. But now, as her condition stabilizes and I move back into my life, I find myself more convicted than ever about the value of being a conscious parent.

Thirty-eight years old, and seemingly healthy, my daughter suffered a massive stroke that nearly took her life and left her paralyzed and unable to speak. Because she received immediate medical care, she is learning to walk and talk again, and I am so grateful. With deficits in affect, memory, speech, hearing, visual perception, reading comprehension and judgment, she has a long road ahead. But she's in good spirits, and we're all envisioning her fully recovered.

I have been able to be an invaluable resource to my daughter and her family during this ordeal and am acutely aware that this would not always have been the case. On the second day post-stroke, when we were fairly certain that she would survive, I had a moment to reflect on our relationship. I wept as I remembered how much tension there had been between us in years past, and how now there is none, just love flowing freely. I can only imagine how wracked with guilt and regret I would have been if she hadn't survived and our relationship remained unhealed.

The truth is that you just never know when something like this might happen. Life is fragile, and we might not have tomorrow to restore our broken relationships. To stay awake is to appreciate that life is a gift we've been given and that it is our spiritual mandate to make the most of the time we have. I am more acutely aware of these truths than ever today, and I feel the need to pass on this urgency because, well, you just never know.

■ ■ ■

*We are all one short breath away from life as we know it being changed forever.*

# · 95 ·

## The Gift of Acknowledgment

*P*art of the human experience seems to be one of self-doubt. No one can successfully navigate all of life's potholes without falling in from time to time, and our self-esteem can collapse then, too. This is why good friends are such a gift, since they love us just as we are, flaws and all. They acknowledge our strengths, forgive our weaknesses and aren't afraid to show their love. Even though mothers know how important it is to feel valued, sometimes it is hard to show our love to our adult children.

I challenged a highly critical mother to tell her daughter two things she appreciated about her during their next visit. The mom protested at first, "You're asking me to be someone I'm not — I'm just not a warm and fuzzy person." But she did want her daughter to stop avoiding her, so she agreed that perhaps she could work on becoming more loving and appreciative. She found this task to be both more difficult and more rewarding than she had anticipated.

The daughter was stunned when her mother complimented her on the chicken salad she had prepared and on the blouse she was wearing during the lunch they shared. She said absolutely nothing for a full minute, but then slowly smiled as she looked quizzically at her mother and said, "Why, thanks, Mom."

What surprised this mother about this encounter was that acknowledging her daughter felt good to her, too. She described the feeling as a softening of the thickness around her heart, a release from some of the constraints of the armor she ordinarily wore around her daughter to protect herself from the sting of rejection. She decided that perhaps it would be worth the risk to discard some of this armor once and for all.

■　■　■

*Giving compliments to or acknowledging*
*the efforts of our adult children is a gift we give not*
*only to them but also to us.*

# · 96 ·

## Expect Less

When we start to parent consciously, we often feel overwhelmed by the sheer volume of all we have to learn and by how slowly we seem to progress. Some days, it seems we haven't learned a thing. Dorothy, a mom of three adult kids, came to her third session looking embarrassed and launched into a barrage of self-deprecating remarks about how terrible she was because she was still interfering in her children's lives and, due to her worries about them, was still not sleeping well. I gently told this mom that she was expecting far more from herself than was realistic, and that it would take time to assimilate the new concepts and change her behavior.

It helps to remember that, as beginners, we're not supposed to be very good at these new skills. When we're learning anything, it takes time before our hard work pays off, and, in the meanwhile, it helps if we can *lower* our expectations of ourselves.

I started taking piano lessons, just for fun, many years after my last lesson. Despite seven years of instruction as a child, as an adult I couldn't even remember how to read music and had to be content with learning simple folk tunes at first. But I determined to practice diligently, and four years later I could play some of the beautiful classical pieces I've always admired. Along the way, I learned to be more patient and gentle with myself.

One thing is for sure: If we don't try new behaviors, nothing will change. So if we start where we are, put one foot in front of the other, accept backsliding as normal, believe in ourselves while keeping our expectations realistic, we *will* learn, and we *will* progress. If we can laugh gently at ourselves along the way, that will be so much the better.

■　■　■

*Remembering to lower our expectations will help us*
*relax and enjoy our learning journey.*

## Taming the Worry Beast

*I*n order to tame the worry beast, we need to learn to put our minds in time-out. Although we may have cause for concern, expending energy obsessing about how we can save our children from certain disaster is seldom useful. Instead, we wind up feeling upset, hopeless and exhausted. Our minds seem to be able to chatter on incessantly, regardless of where we are or what we're doing. These wild beasts must be tamed before they can devour us.

The best way to give our minds a rest is to learn to stay in the present moment, to be fully engaged in whatever we're doing, whether meditating, making love, driving a car, eating lunch or doing laundry. We cannot be focused on the present and be worried at the same time. Worry is always future-oriented and is something that goes on as background noise behind the scenes of our lives. We benefit by learning to "be" more and "think" less.

We can experiment with quieting our minds through focusing on our breathing or on the task in front of us, whether it's washing dishes or pruning rose bushes. We can also study meditation or contemplative prayer. When we hear what Buddhists call our "monkey mind" produce its incessant chatter, we can learn to redirect our focus gently back to the present moment.

We can even get creative and come up with our own solutions. One mom I know decided to give herself just one-half hour per day to worry about her adult children. Throughout the day, when they and their struggles cross her mind, she tells herself, "Not yet—it's not 4:30." When 4:30 does arrive, she stops what she's doing and gives her undivided attention to worrying all she wants. When the clock strikes five, she moves on to another task. The absurdity of this strategy has not escaped this wise mom, and her worry sessions are gradually getting shorter.

■　■　■

*We will be more serene and happy as we learn to tame our*
*"monkey minds" instead of allowing them to control us.*

# · 98 ·

## A Ship in the Port of Serenity

Sometimes I began my Mothers' Group by sharing a reading about parenting adult children, then asking the members to reflect and write for five minutes. A writing tool the moms liked was the Alpha Poem, taught to me by my friend Susan Meyn, L.P.C., an expert on therapeutic writing.

One evening, the theme of the reading was worry. The reading described why worrying is not an act of love and offered positive suggestions of what to do instead, including giving our kids the benefit of the doubt; looking for ways to have fun with them; acknowledging their strengths; and getting the focus off of them by living rich and full lives.

Suzanne, a group member, was worried about her chemically dependent son, who was barely in recovery, teetering on the brink of relapse. An ocean lover, she immediately envisioned herself as a ship traveling the rough seas of addiction. She shared her Alpha Poem:

Weather storms wrapped in the full gear of healthy thinking, heading toward serenity.

Overcome high seas by trusting that my recovery vessel can ride the crests and dips of the chaos known as addiction.

Replenish my supplies of focus and acceptance whenever in a calm port.

Rest in the knowledge that God is in control and my white-knuckled grip never helps.

Yield to the mantras I've learned: One day at a time. Let go and let God. Then I'll find myself in peaceful waters.

■ ■ ■

*Learning that worrying is optional*
*and that we can choose to take positive action*
*to calm ourselves is a great relief.*

## Motherhood—Not a Popularity Contest

*T*wenty-two-year-old Christina came to see me at the urging of her family. She was distrustful of everyone but her mother and barely spoke at first. Slowly I was able to piece together that she was suffering from hallucinations due to her addiction to crystal methedrine. She had dropped out of school, had no friends or hobbies, and left her bedroom only to see me or buy drugs.

A picture unfolded of a disturbed young woman who manipulated her mother into giving her everything she wanted, including the money to buy drugs. I realized that I would have to include Christina's mom in therapy if change were to occur. When mom explained that she spoiled her daughter because she couldn't tolerate her being mad at her, I knew I would have to model effective parenting for this mom or her daughter would likely self-destruct.

I consistently treated Christina in an honest, loving and firm manner and coached her mom to do the same. To increase her effectiveness, mom also began attending NarAnon support group meetings. Amazingly, Christina continued to come for therapy. Medication helped reduce her hallucinations, and, in time, she managed to obtain her G.E.D. But because she continued to see drugs as her best friend and would not follow through with drug treatment recommendations, she couldn't move forward.

I prepared mom to tell her daughter that she must either enter drug treatment or move out of their home. When I told Christina that her mom was getting stronger and would no longer stand by and watch her destroy herself, she assured me, "Oh, my mom will never kick me out." When mom did follow through, her daughter was shocked and outraged but finally agreed to enter treatment. After several months of being clean and sober, she told me, "I'm glad I had two people who cared about me more than I cared about myself. I knew I was going under, but I just couldn't stop myself."

■　■　■

*Sometimes setting firm and unpopular boundaries is*
*the kindest thing we can do for our children.*

## Productive Versus Unproductive Worry

*T*here *is* a place for worry in the lives of mothers of adult children, just not the prominent place that it holds for most of us. Worrying is an adaptive behavior that evolved to help our ancient ancestors stay alert to the potential of predators and strangers. It helped keep them ready to defend themselves and their families. Staying on guard was a life and death matter in prehistoric times.

Rarely are the things we worry about today matters of life or death. In fact, surveys indicate that 85 percent of the things we worry about will have positive outcomes, and, of the 15 percent that don't, we'll handle 80 percent of those situations better than we thought we would.

It can be helpful to learn to distinguish between productive and unproductive worry. Productive worry, as in the case of our ancestors, calls for action. Unproductive worry, on the other hand, is endless, concerning itself with all the what-ifs and worst-case-scenarios we can envision. An example of productive, or good, worrying occurred when my daughter was getting married, and I was worried that I might forget to include some important people on the guest list. This specific concern led me to scour my phone and address books, and to check with my daughter and future son-in-law in order to make certain my list was comprehensive. The worrying was replaced with relief once that task was completed.

An example of unproductive, or bad, worrying, on the other hand, would have occurred if I had stayed awake night after night obsessing that my daughter was marrying the wrong man. This concern could have snowballed into panic and ruined the whole wedding experience. Furthermore, it wouldn't have called for any action, since an expression of concern on my part would have been interpreted by my daughter as unwelcome interference.

■  ■  ■

*Good worry inspires positive action and leads to resolution, while bad worry just makes us sick.*

## Empty Nest as Fertile Ground

*P*enny, a divorced mom of two young adults, reported feeling depressed. "I graduated from college, got married and gave birth to my two sons before I was 25. It's been just the three of us since my divorce ten years ago," she told me. "After I took my younger son to college, I thought I'd be so happy to have time for myself at last, but, instead, all I do is sit and cry. My boys don't need me much anymore. Aside from being their mom, I really don't have a clue who I am."

This lack of personal identity is a common issue for women. Even my 95-year-old aunt told me after her husband died, "I've never lived alone before. I've spent my entire life taking care of my family. Then I knew who I was. Now I have too much time to think, and a lot of what I think about is how lonely I am."

Providing care is the noble and important work of mothers. But if we have done our job well, by the time our kids are young adults, we've mostly worked our way out of that job, leaving us to face ourselves. Along the way, we have neglected our own needs and may not even know what they are. Penny told me, "I've always known what my kids needed even before they knew. When I try to figure out what I want, I have no clue."

I tell clients like Penny when you make a transition into an exciting new stage of life, you don't yet have the map necessary to navigate these uncharted waters. Your empty nest is fertile ground in which new seeds will take hold, put down roots and, in time, grow into magnificent flowers. Meanwhile, this is the time to cultivate an intense curiosity about yourself and embrace your new adventure, tears and all.

■ ■ ■

*Although we may feel lost and afraid when our children leave home, our empty nest provides fertile ground for new growth.*

## The Empty Nest, Part Two: A Call to Dig Deep

*F*or mothers of adult children, the empty nest gives birth to existential questions such as: Who am I? What is the meaning or purpose of my life? What do I want to be when I grow up? Moms often report that they were clear about their identity and purpose when they were raising their kids, but no longer feel important or valuable with their children out of the home. This quandary can hold true even for women with satisfying career paths.

These questions are deeply spiritual (though not necessarily religious) ones, because they are the questions of the spirit, related to our deepest essence. When we were frantically juggling raising children with busy careers, we didn't have the time, energy or inclination to consider such issues. But now we have the opportunity to examine our lives more deeply. We give ourselves a great gift when we step back from the numbing routines of daily life to get to know our deepest desires.

By developing a fascination and curiosity about how to live our very best lives, we can determine what really matters. Then we can live out of the meaning that we discover. One mother I know who lived in the middle of a bustling city reconnected with her childhood love of horses and eventually moved to a small town where she could keep horses. Another mom felt a need for an outlet for all the hands-on nurturing her children no longer needed, so she became a foster grandparent. A third felt a nagging creative urge and signed up at a community college for a poetry class in which she explored the existential themes of her empty nest.

■ ■ ■

*As our children need us less,*
*the challenge and gift of the empty nest is to help us*
*discover more deeply who we really are.*

## Listening to the Wisdom Within

*L*earning to live from the deeper perspective of the soul is much easier said than done for mothers who have always been controlled by the clock and the endless list of chores, errands and drives to basketball games. In order to hear the still, quiet voice of the soul, we must become quiet and slow down our body and mind so that we can hear what's really important.

To the question "What do I really like, value or need?" our mind is likely to tell us either the logical answer or what it thinks will please others. We must learn not to listen solely to our rational mind, our intellect. We are much more than what we think. We can learn to tune into ever-deepening truth and then to act from this heightened awareness. Even small, seemingly inconsequential changes can contribute substantially to the quality of our lives.

One of my friends, newly divorced and the mother of three grown children, decided to remodel her kitchen. She was confused about what colors to use on her walls and countertops. "I think they should probably be green," she said, "because I keep reading that green is a soothing color, and it will blend with all the trees in my backyard. But my realtor friend says I should go more neutral in case I decide to sell. And my mom agrees with her."

I told my friend, "It's your house. What color do *you* want?" When she admitted she had no idea, I suggested she tune out all the "right" answers, go alone to visit model homes, and tune into what pleases her. She called me excitedly a few weeks later to tell me, "The workmen are here putting in my gorgeous Wedgwood blue countertops—I had never even considered blue until I saw it in one of the model homes. Now I'm totally enchanted!"

■ ■ ■

*Learning to listen, trust and then
act on our deep inner experience is the path to an
authentic and satisfying life.*

## Life Is Full of Ups and Downs

*T*hirty-one years ago, after completing graduate school, I was excited to have the opportunity to decorate my first office. I searched for inexpensive artwork and found a framed poster of a photograph of a hundred or more penguins, each waiting patiently in line for their chance to jump off the cliff into the ocean far below. The caption read, "Life is Full of Ups and Downs." I think I am only now beginning to grasp fully the deep wisdom this poster implied.

When my daughter suffered a massive stroke a few years ago, I was grateful beyond words that her life had been saved and that she had the opportunity to recover from the assault on her brain. What I didn't know then was how slow and halting her progress would be. At times, she would even move backward. When this happened, I found myself facing crippling fear and panic, my mind attacking me with worries that she would never get better or was again in danger of stroking. Although her doctors and therapists were not concerned, I lost sleep.

Thankfully, I remembered to pull out my trusty emotional tool kit to help me with my fears. Remembering the lesson of the penguins turned out to be one of the more powerful devices. No lasting change occurs with steady onward and upward motion. It is natural and normal for there to be detours and wrong forks taken. Indeed, life *is* full of ups and downs; however, even two steps forward, one back still results in cumulative progress.

During this time, I worked nearly as hard on achieving peace of mind as my daughter worked on recovering her speech and mobility. As I learned to breathe through the fear and release the panic, I was able to remain peaceful even when my dear daughter was having a hard day, week or month.

■　■　■

*Remembering the natural rhythm of hard days following good days following hard days helps us mothers release our fears about our adult children.*

## Letting Go Feels So Unnatural

When I'm worried about my kids' ability to be responsible and take good care of themselves, I often want to educate or influence them about how I think they should be living their lives. I experience this clutching sensation in the pit of my stomach that seems to compel me to take some kind of action to get them to shape up. In talking with hundreds of mothers, I have found that although the content of our concerns may vary significantly—from addiction to debt to poor partnering—the clutching sensation and the compulsion to intervene are universal experiences for mothers of adult kids.

Learning to let go of control is perhaps the most essential tool we can learn to use. Yet nothing feels quite as unnatural as letting go when we're afraid. Instead, we want to grab hold of the problems we see and hang on for dear life until they're solved. We are learning that these attempts to fix them and their problems don't tend to work. Rather, we alienate or at least annoy our loved ones and drive ourselves crazy in the process. Why is it so hard to let go of the need for control? Because we don't know what will happen if we do, and that fear of the unknown is terrifying.

It helps to remember that it is normal for a mother to want the best for her children. But long ago I lost all but the illusion of control over my children's struggles to grow up. Letting go is about opening to the experiences that await me and them, rather than clamping down and holding on to my plans for their lives. In the process of letting go and accepting that they are on their own journeys, I can move toward the blessed peace of mind that will elude me otherwise.

■ ■ ■

*Although it feels unnatural to let go of trying to solve*
*our adult children's challenges, we'll be far happier if*
*we learn to do so.*

## Get Creative

*L*ois had always been a devoted mother to her now 24-year-old son Derek. She and her husband paid for his college and afterwards let him move back home when he still didn't know what he wanted to do with his life. Although Derek moved out several times, whenever a job or relationship ended he would always return to the comforts of home.

After years of watching her son flounder, the usually patient Lois began to show signs of strain. She had envisioned her empty nest leading to more freedom, financial and otherwise. Instead, continuing to support Derek ate up most of her disposable income. Although pleasant enough, he tended not to work when he lived with his parents and slept most of the day after spending late nights out with friends.

It became clear to Lois that Derek was far more comfortable with their living arrangement than she and her husband were. When she came to therapy, she was feeling resentful and finally admitted that she needed to ask him to move out once and for all, despite the guilt she knew she'd feel. She exclaimed, "He's not trying to 'find himself.' Instead, he's 'found himself' a cushy deal!"

Lois and I strategized, and with her husband by her side she delivered the following speech: "Son, we owe you an apology. We've been treating you as though you were a teenager instead of the grown man you are. By letting you live here rent-free, we have been disrespectful, and we hope you'll forgive us. It's time for you to find your own place so we can all begin to relate as adults. We have cramped your style long enough." Derek forgave his parents, got a job and moved out within the month. Lois and her husband are spending their disposable income in Europe.

■　■　■

*By opening ourselves up to unconventional methods,*
*we may find creative solutions to sticky problems.*

## Spiritual Parenting

Kahlil Gibran says about parenting, "Children come through us but not from us." So if we think of being a parent as a spiritual endeavor, we can choose to believe when our children were born we entered into a sacred contract with them in which we were called to see them as precious and unique souls. Our contract was to help them fulfill their purpose here on earth. If we can accept that they don't belong to us, then we are in a position to help them belong to themselves and find their own place in this world.

We may help our children find their purpose by seeing that they get good educations and are exposed to activities that broaden them and shape their interests. But perhaps even more important than the opportunities we afford them is the quality of our encounters with them, including our ability to perceive them with wonder and reverence no matter whether they become attorneys, forget our birthdays, write novels or go through three divorces.

It is never too late for us to cultivate this spiritual approach to parenting. A powerful shift will occur within us if we practice parenting skills in which we soothe and support, encourage inspiration and creativity, and affirm the inherent value of our adult kids so that they may then place more value on their deep inner yearnings.

Rather than seeing them as "ours," we can think of them as belonging to the world, with us as their hosts or guides as they move along on their journeys. If we envision them as coming to earth to discover their unique purpose, it will be easier for us to remember that we must let them find their own way—detours, mountain tops, deserts, potholes and all.

■　■　■

*Seeing ourselves as spiritual guides allows us to view our adult children with respect for the uniqueness of their souls' journeys.*

# · 108 ·

## Spiritual Parenting, Part Two: Beholding

*I*n order to see our children as spiritual beings, we must learn the art of "beholding," which means seeing without judgment, spirit to spirit. Beholding our children requires us to soften our eyes and see through the eyes of our hearts. The Buddhist priest Thich Nhat Hanh calls this "pure recognition," an attitude of openness, curiosity and simple appreciation. We may then begin to experience our children below the surface, to feel their spirits and to appreciate their preciousness. This deep awareness is a gift to us as well as to them.

Remembering how we feel when we see a new baby, a puppy or a kitten will help us know if we're on the right track. We feel such delight and wonder when we behold these tiny creatures that we just can't take our eyes off of them. This is because their spirits are so unguarded that we can't help but be captivated, and we fall in love almost immediately. In addition, we connect with them on the level of spirit, with no ego involvement. That is, we have no need for them to be anything but who they are.

Later, when they aren't quite as tiny or as cute, and they begin to displease or disappointment us, we begin the gradual transition from spiritual to ego-driven encounters, often losing touch with that perception of luminosity in the process. Consider how common it is to hear new parents speak adoringly about their babies, and how infrequently we hear that same adoration in parents of adult children.

Psychologist Ira Progoff states, "Love depends upon the capacity to reach beneath the surface of persons, to feel and touch the seed of life that is hidden there. And love becomes a power when it is capable of evoking that seed and drawing it forth from its hiding place."

■ ■ ■

*Looking at our adult children through the softened eyes of our hearts will allow us to nourish the seeds of their spirits.*

## Spiritual Parenting, Part Three: Being Present

*P*arenting becomes a spiritual discipline when we practice the art of being present to our children. Being present *to* is not the same as being present *with* our children. Whether we encounter them in person, by phone, text or e-mail, it is far more likely that we are present *with* them than that we are present *to* them. To be present means to be awake and mindful of what is going on within us, our kids and our relationship.

Being present allows us to be aware, without judgment, in the here and now. Instead of reacting impulsively, when we learn to observe our thoughts, feelings and desires to act, we can be more aware of what's called for in any given situation. Many conversations with our adult kids go badly because, instead of just being present to them while they share about their lives, we react by jumping in uninvited to try and fix whatever we see as their problems. The opposite of being present is to be unaware, distracted or absorbed in the whirlwind of our own thoughts or agendas.

Being present invites us to pause inwardly, to take a breath and to check in with ourselves *before* we say or do anything. We can notice our body's sensations and ask, "My stomach is tight. What's that about?" Or, "Why I am so upset about this?" Or even, "Can I be more gentle and loving right now?" This simple practice can make a world of difference. Fundamentally, being present is an act of respect, sending the powerful message to our children that they are worthy of our full and complete attention. We respect them enough to listen deeply to them.

■ ■ ■

*Being present to our adult children means that we stay in touch enough to feel each other's warmth.*

## Not Just a Walk in the Park

*I* spent a morning with my little granddaughter at the park. While keeping an eye on her as she played happily on the playground, I had the chance to observe the scores of young moms watching over their tiny charges. I was once again struck by the enormous responsibility and the sheer volume of time, love, energy and money involved in raising a child.

Taking my own kids to the park when they were small was always a fun outing. I never saw those trips as a sacrifice. As I watched those moms that sunny morning, I saw them dealing with the constant threat of accidents and the occasional skinned knee, and with bruised egos when one child wouldn't let another take her turn with the sandbox toys. They provided drinks and snacks and bread for the ducks. They cheered wildly when their child made it to the top of the jungle gym. As time wore on, they cheerfully contended with runny noses, pre-naptime crankiness and inordinate amounts of sand.

As the moms watched their kids, I watched the moms. My heart filled with pride and appreciation for them, for me, for all of us. It would be easy to dismiss this as simply "mother's work"– after all, it's just what moms do. But I stepped back and, with the perspective of 40 years of parenting, saw the devotion, the tireless and endless sacrifice and the monumental investment in time, sweat and tears that goes with being a mom. Despite these trying times, I was filled with hope for humanity, believing that the light and love that shines forth from each mother during each visit to the park imbues the next generation with the will to go on and make the world a better place.

■ ■ ■

*Mothers of children of all ages deserve kudos for the countless small, selfless gestures of love and sacrifice that they perform without complaint each day.*

## Regression Can Be Normal

*M*ost mothers are familiar with the psychological concept of regression as it relates to children. Regression represents a return to behaviors from an earlier time and occurs when a child is feeling stressed. If a four-year-old only child has to make room for a new baby, she often returns temporarily to infantile behaviors such as wanting a bottle or wetting her pants.

A smart mom sees these signs as normal reactions to her daughter having to give up her princess status and, rather than shaming her, gives her special alone time, a chance to help with her new sibling, or her very own baby doll. I remember regressing when our family moved to a new town when I was 11. I asked for, was given and became instantly attached to a realistic baby doll more appropriate for a child of seven.

I've experienced first-hand that regression can occur in mothers, too. When my daughter suffered a stroke, she became very childlike for a time, and I found myself reverting to long-forgotten modes of parenting, including giving unsolicited advice, hovering, being intrusive and even talking baby talk. Initially, this behavior was not entirely inappropriate, given the extent of her disability. But, even as her condition began to improve, I continued to treat her like a little girl.

One night, after she had begun to regain her ability to speak, I called my daughter and said, "I just couldn't stand to go to bed without saying goodnight to my little girl." She responded slowly but clearly, "I'm not your little girl. I'm 38." I was glad to discover that her ability to hold her own with me seemed to be intact. I decided not to expect too much of myself at such a difficult time.

■ ■ ■

*When our children are enduring difficult circumstances, we can forgive ourselves for reverting to old parenting techniques we thought we'd given up forever.*

## Empathy, Not Sympathy

*M*any mid-life mothers feel shut out of their adult children's lives and yearn to be let in, while others feel like their kids' main source of emotional support and yearn for more separateness. At one of my mothers' groups, the evening's topic was how to be there emotionally for our children, if invited, without losing our sanity in the process. We developed this list of guidelines to help us care about our children *and* ourselves.

1. Accept their emotions as valid and not in need of minimizing or "fixing." Allow our children to have their own emotional experiences without judgment. Just because I would be upset if my dog peed on the carpet doesn't mean my daughter has to share my discontent.

2. Distinguish between being there for them emotionally and being emotional *for* them. We can bear their pain *with* them, but not *for* them. Actively listening — by validating them or asking clarifying questions — can feel deeply satisfying to them.

3. Allowing them to learn through adversity is a great gift. If their situation calls for a solution, rather than offering one, we can affirm their ability to handle their problem and if they are interested, help them explore possible solutions.

4. Judiciously share experiences of our own that may be similar to theirs in order to show them that we understand. When my son was angry and hurt because of his son's disrespect, I shared how I coped with that same situation when he was a teen. This disclosure helped him realize how his son might be feeling and not take his rejection so personally. We had a nice moment sharing our parenting trials.

5. Strive to maintain our serenity in the midst of their life storms. It doesn't mean we love them more if we get upset, too.

6. Allow them to be there for us on occasion. This helps equalize and legitimize a relationship between two adults.

■ ■ ■

*We can best be there emotionally for our adult children by offering empathy rather than sympathy.*

## Siblings: Mars versus Venus

*D*uring a visit with a friend, the mother of two grown daughters who were in graduate school in distant states told me, "Well, Barb's spring break is over. She's headed back to school, and I'm trying to rest up before Laurie arrives tomorrow because that'll be an entirely different experience." We laughed as we shared how dissimilar our children are.

"Even though they're both girls, I swear it's like they're from different planets," my friend said. She described her older daughter Barb as easy-going and helpful, with lots of friends she visits while staying with her parents. Laurie, on the other hand, complains constantly, is more demanding and has few friends. "She's always been high-maintenance and seems to hang around waiting for us to entertain her," my friend told me.

She then admitted, "When they were little, I overprotected Laurie because she had asthma. I also tried to get her to be more like Barb which I know now really hurt her perception of herself. I feel really bad about those things, but there is nothing I can do to change them other than try and do a better job now. So these days I prepare myself before their visits. I've come to accept that my relationship with each of them is different because they're so different.

"I try to keep in mind that they need different things from me and that it helps all of us if I can meet those needs, as long as I don't hurt myself in the process. So, for example, I free up more time to spend with Laurie, and I offer her more validation and affirmation than I do her sister. It gets trickier when we're all together at Christmas, but I just try to stay awake and conscious, to have loving and authentic communication with them, and to enjoy them both. It still amazes me that they grew up in the same family!"

· · ·

*Staying aware of each of our adult children's unique traits allows us to adapt our parenting styles and have successful, though different, relationships with each of them.*

## Just Enough Guilt

When sharing with friends who are also mothers of adult children, I often tell tales on myself, complete with good-natured self-deprecation along the lines of, "Oh, I can be such a drama queen!" or "You know what a control freak I can be." Often my friends jump in immediately and try to rescue me. "Oh, you are not," or "Quit being so hard on yourself," they tell me. This interchange is usually followed by an interesting dialogue in which I try and convince them that it's actually a sign of healthy self-esteem that I can make fun of myself. This is a paradoxical truth: The more I face and understand my deficits, the less I'm held captive by them and the more I'm free to love myself.

Remember, in the story of "Goldilocks and the Three Bears," Goldilocks went to the Bears' house when they were out for a walk, looking for food and a place to rest. She had three choices each of porridge, chairs to sit on, and beds to sleep in. In each case, one was too much, another was not enough, and the third, always Baby Bear's, was just right. Such is the case with guilt: When we have too much, we feel crippled by our self-hatred. If we have too little, or more precisely, haven't faced the ways we have been less than perfect mothers, then we're always defending our position and trying to prove that we're in the right.

This, then, is the paradox about facing and healing guilt: Only if we have just enough, or, to put it another way—healthy—guilt are we able to face the truth about ourselves and our children and still feel good about us and them. The goal is not to feel as though we've been perfect mothers, for there is no such thing. Rather, we can only forgive ourselves when we understand and accept how we've messed up.

■   ■   ■

*We can only really love ourselves when we have just enough guilt to accept our imperfections.*

## The Courage to Be Separate

*I*t takes courage to be a conscious mother. Nearly all of the mothers I encounter are worried about at least one of their children. We don't know what it would ever take to get our sons not to be mad at us, or to become financially stable, or our daughters to stop abusing drugs, or to settle down at last. We spend countless hours ruminating about these issues, and we talk endlessly to our friends and family about what, if anything, we can do to help.

What hurts the most to admit, and takes the most courage to face, is that there is usually little if anything we can do other than to learn how to be okay even when they're not. This may seem like a radical idea: "How can I let myself be happy when my child is struggling? It seems disloyal and selfish for me not to be suffering, too." The truth is that it is an act of emotional health to know our limitations and to be content with them. We are not our children; they are not us. Although our lives may intertwine with theirs, our lives are not their lives. We are free to live our own best lives regardless of how they choose to live theirs.

During lunch with a friend I see only occasionally, I asked how her 40-year-old daughter was doing. With a smile, she told me, "She's still on disability, not working, abusing painkillers and dreaming of being a rock star." Then I asked, "How are you doing?" She answered "I'm actually doing well. I've really got it now that I've done all she'll let me do to help her. I love her, and we get along quite well. She knows I'll pay for professional help if she's ever ready to accept it. Meanwhile, my work and marriage are going great, and I make sure to have some fun every day."

■ ■ ■

*Flourishing when our adult children are struggling doesn't mean we don't love them; it just means we love ourselves, too.*

## The Good-Enough Mother

*T*he expression "Be careful what you ask for. You just might get it," comes to mind when I reflect on the honest and authentic relationships I now have with my adult children. After years of dreaming about, modeling, requesting and finally receiving gentle honesty and mutual respect, sometimes it seems I've created a monster. I've discovered that love sometimes hurts, even while it blesses, because of the way it can pinch my ego.

In fact, two benefits I receive from my relationship with my children are the twin gifts of more humility and less ego. I admit it. I'm human: I love it when my kids express gratitude for all the things I've done (and do) for them. I could do without them telling me the hurtful things I've done (or do). It stretches me to accept that, in authentic relationships, you can't expect appreciation without occasional censure.

Fortunately, when my children point out my acts of thoughtlessness, intrusiveness or attempts to control, they do so gently. Even though what they tell me may sting, I see it as an investment in the foundation of our relationship rather than as an attack. I'm glad that they aren't afraid of me, since I do my best not to get defensive. And these gentle ego-shavings are opportunities for growth, notches on my ever-expanding humility belt.

I used to see myself as a nearly perfect mother. Now I realize that, when I interact with my kids, I often step on some boundary or another. I am learning to be satisfied with being a good-enough mother, accepting that I'm flawed and always striving to improve. I use my humility belt not to flog my value as a mother but to rein in my ego.

■　■　■

*When we choose to allow our children to point out our shortcomings, they can teach us to be satisfied with being less than perfect.*

## Being *Too* Available

*M*y friend Diana explained how she could never share any of her hurts, insecurities or questions about boys, friends or sex with her mother, who was always overwhelmed by her own life. Diana remembers thinking, "If I ever have a daughter, I'll make sure she can tell me anything, and I'll always be there for her."

Diana and her husband were indeed blessed with two daughters, both now in their mid-20s, and, in keeping with her pledge, this mom worked hard to provide a safe haven for her girls. Reflecting on her parenting style now, she realizes that perhaps she went from one extreme to the other, since her approach has been to be largely selfless. She is exhausted from riding the emotional roller coaster with her girls as they climb the slippery slope toward maturity.

Diana relayed a rather typical night in which she received three nearly hysterical phone calls from her younger daughter, a graduate student living 3000 miles away. The last call came at 1:30 a.m., and wakened my friend from a sound sleep. Each of these tearful calls had to do with her daughter's latest relationship woes, and each lasted more than 45 minutes. Diana knew that nothing ever changed after these phone calls, and that her daughter would return to her boyfriend until he spit her back out again, followed by more phone calls to her mom. Meanwhile, Diana lost another night's sleep.

Feeling increasingly frustrated as she realized she had become a part of the problem, Diana decided to tell her daughter about *her* needs and informed her not to call again after 8:00 p.m., except in extreme emergencies like being hospitalized. She also told her that she would only be willing to listen to her problems with her boyfriend if she was ready to take positive action. Although she suffered from a little guilt, my friend felt mostly relieved.

■　■　■

***Sometimes, we can be too available***
***to our adult children.***

## The Courage to Be Me

*O*ne of our biggest challenges as mothers is to find a way to maintain our own hope and joy even when our children don't seem to have much. It doesn't do us or them any good if we stay entrenched in their lives of dysfunction or despair. Remember how flight attendants instruct us in case of emergency to put on our own oxygen masks before our children's? The principle is similar no matter what difficult situation we're facing: We can only help our children if we ourselves have enough oxygen, peace of mind and joy.

Susan, the mother of two sons with drug and alcohol addictions, is working on finding herself again after years of being lost in the grips of despair as she worked valiantly to help young men who didn't want to be helped. She offered to share the following reflective piece to illustrate her search for her former joyous self:

"It may be a family disease—alcoholism, drug addiction—but I don't have to be in the ambulance or the treatment room. I don't even have to be on call anymore. I can set my feet on a separate path, remembering that once I lived my life untouched by these dynamics. Once there was a me who loved dancing with my bedpost, who idolized the couples on American Bandstand and a me who accompanied the youth choir and played five-part inventions at Bach festivals. Even after I married, there was a me who reveled in playing with my young sons at the water park.

"Once there was a me who looked to the future with hope and positive expectations. That me is around here somewhere. I just need to bring her out of storage—freshen her makeup, update her clothing and breathe new life into her."

■　■　■

*Regardless of the state of being of our grown kids,
taking the time to search consciously for a more
joyous life is an effort well worth making.*

## Letting Our Illusions Go

*I*n our search for wholeness, one of the hardest skills we must master is to let go of our illusions. When people ask us how our children are doing, we want to be able to mean it when we answer, "Great!" We want to believe that they're flourishing in all areas. We want to feel close to them and their families and to have frequent warm, loving gatherings. This doesn't seem too much to ask.

But what I keep hearing from many of the mothers I know are stories like the following: "I can't even get him to tell me which Easter service he's going to so I'll know when to put in the roast." And "She still won't risk rocking the boat with her husband who doesn't like me. So I've never even met my youngest grandchild, who's almost three."

Others tell me, "My son relates to me only as his babysitter. If I'm pretending, I can tell friends that our families are close because I see my grandkids a lot. But my son rarely gives me the time of day unless he wants something from me, and that hurts." And "Sure, I can brag about my daughter, the successful attorney. But the truth is that I know not to call her after 7 p.m., because she'll be too drunk to talk."

It's a relief to know that we're not alone. To our outer circle of friends and work associates, we can answer the question of how our kids are doing in vague half-truths, since they're likely just making pleasant conversation. But to our inner circle, it's good for the soul to let our illusions go and tell the whole truth. More often than not, they'll respond with their own challenging situations.

■  ■  ■

*Because illusion imprisons us, the more we can let*
*our illusions die and accept the truth about our adult*
*kids, the more free we'll feel.*

## Great Job, Honey!

*A*s we continue to become more conscious parents, one reality we must face is that although we may continue to influence the lives of our adult children through subtle, skillful planting of seeds, we will seldom be given any credit for actions that take root. If we were fully actualized, just knowing that we've done a good job might be sufficient reward. But most of us need and deserve pats on the back — we just can't expect to get them from our adult kids.

My friend Marilyn told me how her daughter Amanda was constantly worrying about her son Sam's grades. Sam had a rude awakening when he moved into a challenging high school program from a lenient middle school, which hadn't assigned grades. Sam simply wasn't used to working very hard and far preferred text messaging his friends.

For months, when Amanda complained to her mom about Sam's poor grades, Marilyn just listened, offering comments like, "Maybe he's still just getting used to the new regimen," or "That sounds hard, honey." Amanda's attempts to help seemed to consist of asking Sam if he had finished his homework, to which he always answered "yes." Gradually, from a loving and detached place, Marilyn offered some variation on this thought: "I wonder if he might benefit from some incentives or more hands-on supervision." Then she just sat back and waited.

Months later, Amanda told her mom, "Well I finally got mad and took action. Sam has lost his phone privileges until his grades come up, and I'm monitoring his homework every night. He told me he hates it but is glad I'm doing it." Marilyn was tempted to say, "I'm sure glad you're finally doing what I suggested months ago." But, instead, she responded, "Great job, honey. You're such a good mom." My response to Marilyn's story? "Great job, my friend. You're such a good mom!"

■ ■ ■

*Learning not to expect appreciation for our efforts to help is a sign of mature parenting, as is asking for that same affirmation from our friends.*

## Love Is a Verb

*V*anessa was troubled by her adult son's immaturity and by her strained relationship with him. She told me, "As a mother, I feel terrible admitting this, but I don't feel much love for him anymore. When he was little, he was so easy to love, but now…" She paused and began quietly weeping. "He just won't do anything to help himself, and then he takes out his disappointment in himself on me. So now I dread seeing his name in my caller ID. When we're together, I can't wait till I can leave. I must be the only mother in the world who feels like this—I just hate it."

I assured Vanessa this situation is more common than she might think, and I explained that when we think of love as a noun—a feeling of warmth and fondness—we're bound to feel disappointed by its absence when we feel angry or hurt. If, on the other hand, we think of love as a verb—a choice that we can make and display through action—then we have a much better chance to be at peace. We may even find that deep feeling of affection returning.

Vanessa made a choice to begin to love her son through the actions she took, and these small intentional acts helped her feel better about her son. She knew her actions were helping him, too, even if in nearly imperceptible ways. She began smiling at and hugging him whenever they got together, finding something to compliment him on during each conversation, putting herself in his shoes in order to have compassion for his struggles, biting her tongue when she felt compelled to offer advice, and sending regular emails or cards of encouragement or appreciation. At our last session she told me, "My son might not be much better, but I feel like a new person."

■　■　■

*Rather than seeing love as a feeling,*
*it helps us and our adult children when we see love*
*as a decision we can make every day.*

## Being Tested

Shortly after writing my essay about love being a verb, I had an opportunity to learn the lesson I was teaching (again). God really does, as they say, have a sense of humor. When my son did something that disappointed me terribly, I behaved badly.

I rarely ask my adult children for help but this time asked my son to help me with something I could not do myself. I gave him every opportunity to say no, clarified his willingness to proceed and made plans accordingly. One night, when he told me he wasn't going to help me after all, I became so enraged that I thought the fire department would have to be summoned to extinguish the flames shooting from my ears. The best I could do was to get off the phone before I started saying things I knew I would regret.

I kept my distance for two weeks, stoking the fire of my rage with thoughts of all I'd done for my son over the years, combined with especially hurtful examples of his thoughtlessness. But in the stillness of those sleepless nights, I kept hearing the phrase "love is a verb." At first I mocked and ignored it. My son had disappointed me terribly; I deserved to be mad; and I didn't want to love him, at least not yet.

Gradually, the volume of the venom softened as an antidote appeared. Though I still wasn't feeling loving, I decided to take action. I called my son and expressed my hurt feelings in an appropriate manner. My son listened, and my wound began to heal. Now I realize that taking those two weeks away was an act of love, since it represented a decision not to exact retribution. Come to think of it, maybe I didn't do so badly after all.

■ ■ ■

*Although it is normal to feel hurt and angry when our adult children act in selfish or thoughtless ways, we can still choose to take the high road.*

## Do Your Best and Leave the Rest

*T*here are days when I'm certain that if there were a contest for World's Worst Mother I'd win the trophy hands down. I can be impatient, distracted and emotionally unavailable. Several times, my daughter has told me about important medical tests she has scheduled, and I have promptly forgotten about them until she announced the results.

One year I only remembered my out-of-state grandson's birthday on his actual birthday, and his card and present arrived late. Sometimes I have trouble concentrating on the details of my son's stories about the deals he's made and incentive prizes he's won. Also, if I don't want to miss the television show I'm watching, I don't always answer the phone when family members call.

When I talk with other moms, they tell me similar stories. They say I'm too hard on myself. I guess it's true: I do tend to believe that a good mother has infinite patience, a memory like an elephant, and an endless fascination with everything going on in her children's lives. Maybe there are some moms like that out there, but I'm not one of them.

I do love and care about my children and their families, but I love and care about myself, too. I'm learning that's the way it should be. It's okay for me to set limits on my availability, and I don't have to remember every little detail of their lives in order to qualify as a good mom. Most importantly, I don't have to feel guilty when I mess up — making mistakes is my birthright. All I want is to do my best and leave the rest.

■  ■  ■

*Always putting our family members' needs ahead of our own isn't healthy — we can care for ourselves and still be available to them.*

## Lessons in Unexpected Places

*M*y granddaughter Sheryl, six years old at this writing, is one of my muses. She has such a zest for life that I love watching the world through her wonder-filled eyes. Yesterday I laughed uproariously as she splashed in the pool with her mom and brother, continually shrieking with delight as they tried to see who could stay upright on their beach balls.

Sheryl is the only person in the world who literally does a dance when she sees me, and I'm not the only one she's thrilled to see. Despite how overwhelming life must seem at times for this little soul, she still moves toward each person and experience with curiosity and excitement. Although sometimes a bit cautious, she forges ahead as any great adventurer would.

Because she is present to all of her emotions, Sheryl can go to dark places at times, too. Recently, she got into my car with her mom and a scowl a mile long, explaining, "Grammy, I'm not very happy because I didn't get to finish your Mother's Day card." I attempted to console her to no avail. While my daughter and I chatted, Sheryl pouted silently all the way to the play we were attending.

But within minutes of the beginning of the play, Sheryl was smiling again. Before long, she was shrieking with delight, fully present to this experience. At the intermission, she turned to me with a lilt in her voice, saying, "Grammy, after all this silliness, I'm not feeling disturbing anymore." The next time I felt dark and "disturbing," I remembered this interchange with Sheryl, turned on my favorite upbeat music, and within a short time lifted my gloomy mood.

■　■　■

*If we pay close attention, we can learn important life lessons from the most unexpected of sources.*

## Never Say Never

*I*t helps to pay attention to the ways in which our language shapes our reality. "Always" and "never" are two words that can do much damage. My friend Anne told me a story in which her ability to detach and her sense of humor helped free herself from the suffering triggered by her adult daughter Alicia, who had a tendency to blame Anne for her own misery, no matter what the cause. For example, when Alicia felt hurt after her unsolicited attempt to help her sister was rebuffed, she turned her hurt feelings into anger at her mother who had nothing to do with the situation. Alicia accused Anne of favoring her sister and then refused to speak to her mother for days.

Previously, Anne would have tried frantically to convince Alicia of her love for her, to no avail. This time, having ceased this fruitless endeavor, she became furious at her daughter and stewed for hours as she built her case against Alicia: "She never appreciates what I do for her. She always blames me for the messes she creates because my love is the most secure thing in her life. I've always let her get away with treating me this way. She's always been like this, and I guess she will never change."

After ruminating for 24 hours, Anne was disheartened to observe that, though she felt justified in her anger, she was still suffering. She decided to free herself from the tyranny of "Never and Always Land." Instead of continuing to generalize, Anne disciplined her mind to think only about the current situation. She expressed and released her sadness and anger, recognized this incident as part of a chronic pattern, remembered not to take it personally, and reminded herself that Alicia does express appreciation at times. Finally, Anne created this wry guideline: "I will never use the words 'never' and 'always' because they are never true and they always make me feel worse!"

■ ■ ■

*Using absolute words constricts us and causes us to
suffer, while humor releases us from these binds.*

# · 126 ·

## The Disease to Please

*F*rom early childhood, females are socialized to please others. Many of us have trouble saying "No" when asked to do things we don't want to do. Raised to be agreeable and to put others' needs before our own, we were more tuned in to our children's needs than to our own. Stirring in the guilt we often felt from working outside the home allowed us to concoct the perfect recipe for children who got angry if they didn't get what they want.

This "disease to please" isn't cured when our children reach adulthood. One evening, Beth explained to our mothers' group how her son—an angry, alcohol-abusing 30-year-old—came to her and her husband begging for help. His car had broken down (again), and he didn't have the repair money. While restraining themselves from giving him money, they did loan him their extra car. We expressed concern about this loophole when Beth told us no time limit had been set for the car's return.

After four months, during which time Beth's son never mentioned his intention to return the car, we gently reminded Beth that the title, registration and insurance were in her name, as would be the liability if he were to get into an accident. She admitted being afraid about the liability but more afraid that, if they set any limits, her son would become so enraged that he would cut them out of his life.

As she began to understand how she was being held hostage by her fears and her son's sense of entitlement, Beth leaned on us to help her strengthen her resolve. Finally, she took a deep breath and chose a reasonable deadline for the car's return. She realized she wanted to take this action, without any knowledge of the outcome, because it was the right thing to do for all involved. We cheered her courage.

■　■　■

*When our effectiveness with our adult children is hampered by our desire to have them like us, then it's time to get to work on our recovery from this "disease to please."*

## A Tale of Two Mothers

*L*inda is the mother of Jeff, a 22-year-old with a history of addiction. Before entering treatment, her son destroyed one of her vehicles, was expelled from college, stole money and credit cards, and put Linda and her husband through hell. When Jeff agreed to enter a six-month treatment program, his mom was enormously relieved.

But Linda soon found her peace of mind abandoning her. She constantly worried about relapse and analyzed each communication from Jeff, wondering if he was lying to her. Even though all indications were that he was committed to his new way of life, Linda became increasingly anxious as her son's release date drew near. Our group gently told her that her serenity seemed inextricably bound to Jeff's sobriety.

Margaret is the mother of Jim, a 30-year-old alcoholic whose addiction had cost him his marriage, several jobs, and even his freedom, since he had been in jail several times. Six months earlier, he agreed to get sober (again) in order to see if he and his ex-wife could reconcile. He began to attend daily Alcoholics Anonymous meetings, moved back in with his wife and three kids, and began family counseling.

Margaret told us that her friends had called excitedly. "Aren't you thrilled?" they asked, "Isn't this what you've been dreaming of?" She answered, "No, not really. Just for today I'm happy for him, and I hope and pray for the best. But I understand the power of addiction, so I know there are no guarantees. I was fine before he got sober, and I'll be fine if this doesn't last." Three months later, Jim relapsed, and the marriage was over for good. Margaret reported, "Of course I'm sad, especially for my grandkids who love their daddy so much. But I still have the same great life, so I'm doing just fine."

■ ■ ■

*When we learn how not to attach our peace of mind*
*to our children's behavior, we can be serene*
*in the midst of any storm.*

## Stop-Worrying Tool Kit

*I*t is normal for even the calmest mother to worry occasionally about the welfare of her children. In times of crisis, our brains are hard-wired to solve problems quickly, and productive worrying often results in practical solutions for handling challenging situations. But there is nothing productive about worrying chronically. In fact, we can "worry ourselves sick." If we learn to use tools to manage our worrying, then it won't ruin our lives. A few of these tools are as follows:

- Compartmentalization—we can choose to put our worries aside and distract ourselves so that we can go to work, run errands, even have a nice evening out while rarely thinking of our children. We human beings have an amazing capacity to put aside what is bothering us. As long as this compartmentalization doesn't result in pathological denial, this is an important tool to cultivate.

- Time limits—we can set aside one period a day of up to 30 minutes during which we do all of our worrying. This method requires us to be vigilant about our thought processes so that, when we catch ourselves worrying, we can discipline our minds by deciding, "I will deal with this during my worry time, not now."

- God Box/ Worry Box—we can purchase a pretty container (or even decorate a shoe box) and cut an opening in the top. Whenever we can't seem to stop worrying about something, we can write it on a piece of paper and deposit the slip of paper in our God/Worry box. This is a symbolic way of letting go of those situations over which we have no control. If we have a faith system, we can turn our worries over to God. If we don't have a faith system, we can call it a Letting Go box and still make the symbolic gesture of letting go of that which we can't control.

■ ■ ■

*Since we suffer when our lives are consumed by concerns about our children, we can help ourselves by developing tools to help us stop worrying.*

## When Will I Learn?

When my friend arrived at my house, she was clearly distraught. "He broke my heart again," she told me through her tears. Because I had known her a long time, I knew that she meant her 30-year-old son. "When will I learn? I really believed him this time — he told me he'd change his work schedule so he could fly in for my 50th."

She went on to explain how she'd told him long ago how much it would mean to her if he came. Every time they talked on the phone he would assure her he was working on getting the time off. "I wanted so desperately to believe him that I guess I just conveniently forgot about all the other times he has disappointed me," she said. Then, with the party just two weeks away, she learned he wouldn't be able to come. She complained that he had the nerve to say she shouldn't have gotten her hopes up "because it was never a sure thing."

She realized he probably didn't even try to get the time off. "I constantly give him the benefit of the doubt," she told me. "I ask virtually nothing of him, and then, during the few times I have needed something, he has let me down. I hate to admit it, but my son is immature and selfish."

My heart went out to my friend as I watched her come to terms with how her son is, as opposed to how she wishes he were. We love our children and want to see only the best in them, so it is painful to see them as they are. But our peace of mind requires us to take off our rose-colored glasses, because expectations equal disappointment. If we have realistic expectations, we won't be nearly as disappointed when they aren't met.

■　■　■

*The more we can keep our expectations in line with reality, the less we will have to keep riding the roller coaster of dismay and disillusionment.*

## Pain is Inevitable, Suffering Optional

"*L*ife is difficult" are the first three words in Scott Peck's book The Road Less Traveled. Since we seem to think that life will go smoothly if we treat others well, this concept proves confounding for most of us. When things don't go as we planned, we feel shocked and dismayed. If we can learn to accept that life is meant to be difficult, we can feel our feelings and let them go. We won't suffer when our hopes and dreams don't line up with reality. We can confront and change the sources of our suffering, which include:

- Belief that the pain is unbearable and must be avoided.
- Victim mentality that makes us wonder "Why me?"
- Expectations that don't line up with reality.
- Attachment to specific outcomes – e.g., "If I treat him well, he will treat me well."

At her final session, a mom I had worked with for some time told me "My children are actually doing pretty much the same as they were when we began, maybe even a little worse. My son's drinking is still a big problem, and he won't get help. My daughter is still angry at me much of the time. But I feel completely different. Of course, I feel sad about the choices they keep making, but because I've learned how to observe and accept rather than attach myself to the pain, I'm no longer miserable."

Further, she explained how she stopped trying to change them, stopped blaming herself and mostly stopped worrying. Instead of allowing herself to suffer, she had chosen to create a "wonderful life" for herself rather than wait for her children to change. She told me, "I've learned that I don't have to define myself by their successes or failures. I feel a sense of freedom, and I'm thankful to my kids for being such great teachers."

■　■　■

*Learning to embrace, accept, and release emotional pain can free us from our suffering.*

## Doing Nothing Can Mean Everything

We mothers have spent most of our adult years tending to the needs of others. It doesn't come naturally to give to ourselves. In addition, our society promotes perpetual busyness and teaches us to relegate rest and rejuvenation to one vacation a year. We could perhaps more aptly meet the demands of busy lives if we took time to rest and reconnect with ourselves every week.

Years ago, after reading Wayne Muller's inspiring book, Sabbath, I decided to make at least part of every Sunday a day of rest. Even when I hear the voices of all my unfinished tasks growling at me, I guard this time ferociously and have come to see it as sacred. I begin the day by sitting still, outside if possible and ask myself what I really need to nourish my soul. Some weeks I go to church; other times I don't leave the house. I try and stay away from television and newspapers. I turn the ringers off on the phones and only check email once. I usually don't schedule social events, and then only if they are fun or uplifting.

Yesterday, I napped, daydreamed, ate homemade soup, read a novel and meditated. On other Sundays, I've worked on a scrapbook, taken a walk or called someone I miss. At bedtime, if I can't point to a single task I've completed, I consider the day a success. Even for just a few hours, resting in the stillness nourishes me. I don't solve any of the world's problems or even my own. But I know that when I get up the next day to go to work I will have energy and enthusiasm that I wouldn't have otherwise, and that's accomplishment enough for me.

■  ■  ■

*A day of rest is an important antidote to a mother's*
*depletion of body, mind and spirit.*

## Listening Below the Surface

*M*y client Marilyn shared with me that sometimes it just seems she like she can't say anything right to her daughter. "We can be having a perfectly fine conversation and then out of the blue she gets annoyed and snippy," Marilyn told me, "I feel frustrated because she won't ever talk about what irritates her. I feel like I'm walking on eggshells around her."

She described a time when they were talking on the phone about her grandson's summer plans. Marilyn said she asked for probably the third time in as many weeks if her daughter had signed him up for swimming lessons yet. That's when her daughter barked at her. "Why do you keep bringing this up? I'll get to it when I can," hanging up on her. Stunned by this behavior, Marilyn explained, "She knows how important it is for him to take those lessons, because I have a pool and am a nervous wreck when he visits. It seems like she just doesn't care about my feelings."

I told Marilyn, "Oh, she cares about you, all right. Otherwise, your seemingly insignificant remarks wouldn't get such a rise out of her." I asked her to put herself in her daughter's shoes and try to understand how she might have *interpreted* the words as implying a critical message: that she is a negligent parent because she hasn't taken care of this task. If it hurt to think her mother sees her as irresponsible, it might make sense that she lashed out.

After hearing that, Marilyn first reacted defensively, telling me her daughter shouldn't take her remarks so personally, because she's just trying to safeguard her grandson. Eventually she was able to understand as she remembered feeling the same way with her own critical mother. "I guess I'm going to have to be more aware of how important my approval is to her—her life is hard enough without me making it worse. I won't ask again about the swimming lessons. Maybe I can start teaching my grandson to swim."

· · ·

*Becoming aware of the implied message—that is, how our children interpret our words—can go a long way toward improving communication.*

## Mothers and Daughters

*I* am often struck by how different an experience it is to be the mother of a daughter than the mother of a son. Even though my son was a handful and challenged me greatly when he was growing up, I see now that my relationship with my daughter has always been far more complicated. The following factors contribute to this common phenomenon:

1. Our daughters, by virtue of their more affiliative natures, tend to value emotional closeness more than sons. Mothers and daughters tend to talk more often and for longer periods of time. We enjoy chatting even without an agenda.

2. Mothers are interested in the intimate details of our daughters' lives, and we may know more about them than their fathers, husbands and even friends. We want to know every word spoken during each doctor's visit when they are pregnant. We are interested in where they got their new outfit, how our grandson did on his math test, and whether their friend's marriage will survive. To us, being interested in the smallest details of their lives is a sign of caring and closeness.

3. Because of our access to more information, there are infinite things on which we may feel compelled to comment. Complications ensue because, while we think our involvement stems from caring, our daughters often see it as meddling and critical. The close connection which allows these conversations to occur is, therefore, fraught with danger to that very closeness.

4. Because we share genders, we tend to see our daughters as extensions of us rather than as separate beings. Therefore, we tend to be harder on them than on our friends or even our sons. Because our approval means everything to them, attempts on our part to help our daughters present themselves in their best light tend to be met with hurt feelings and anger.

■   ■   ■

*In order to safeguard our close relationships with our dear daughters, we must stay aware of the delicate balance between closeness and intrusiveness.*

## Why Weight?

*A*s a child, despite the fact that my involvement in sports kept me slim and healthy, my mother was obsessed with what I ate and my weight. If I gained a few pounds, she insisted that I diet. I was never thin enough to please her. I perceived my mom's purported attempts to help me as an indictment of my personhood. I know now that I was a beautiful, slim young girl. But because of my mom's obsessive focus, at sixteen I actually believed I had the biggest rear end of anyone in the world.

When I gained weight during my first pregnancy, my mom panicked. She talked about dieting whenever she visited and sent me newspaper clippings about dieting or health dangers. I interpreted her actions as telling me, "You are not okay the way you are." The feeling of shame that accompanied these words would, of course, draw me back to the refrigerator.

One year, after I had learned in therapy about my right to define how people treat me, I screwed up my courage and told my mom, "When you talk to me about my weight, I feel guilty and ashamed. I don't want you to mention my weight ever again." Although she eventually honored my request, I know she never felt any differently. I felt relieved and empowered, but my heart still hurt.

My mom lacked empathy: She couldn't put herself in my shoes and understand how hurtful her opinion of me was. With the wisdom of maturity, I know now that she loved me and cared about my health. But I also know that she was trying to control and change me because, if I wasn't perfect in her eyes, I reflected badly on her. All I yearned for was to feel loved and accepted. If I had felt that way, I might not have struggled so much with overeating.

· · ·

*When moms tell their children what they do not approve of, we hear the words, "I don't love you, because you're not okay the way you are."*

## The Importance of Staying Connected

*I*t seems that it has become normal to be lonely in the United States. According to several surveys, there is a definite trend toward living more isolated lives today. Two surveys were conducted in 1985 and 2007 by the National Opinion Research Center at the University of Chicago. They found some striking differences. In 1985, the average American had three people in whom to confide matters that were important to them. By 2007, the number had dropped to two. One in four had no close confidants at all. Fewer contacts come from clubs, churches and neighbors, as people rely more on family. The percent of people who confide only in family increased from 57 to 80.

Given that research has linked social isolation and loneliness to mental and physical illness, these statistics have far-reaching implications. I have noticed a microcosm of this phenomenon in my practice: During my years as a psychotherapist, there has been a noted decrease in the quality of social support reported by my mostly female clientele. Many of my clients see the therapeutic relationship as their most intimate. I strongly encourage them to explore and develop close friendships.

I really don't know where I'd be without my dear close friends. I don't have just one best friend. I have four or five in whom I can confide my deepest desires and darkest secrets. If one isn't available, another likely is. Sometimes I share my concerns or vent my frustration about my adult children and grandchildren. I also have six or seven people, including some extended family, whom I consider close friends, but not as close as the inner tier. It is because I have so many nurturing friendships that I don't have to rely on either of my children to be a regular source of emotional support. I feel richly blessed.

■　■　■

*For mothers who worry about their adult children, the emotional support of friends is a necessity, not a luxury.*

## So Much to Change, So Little Time

*I* had one of those "aha!" experiences while I watched my daughter fuss with her little girl—six at the time—as they prepared for a concert at my granddaughter's school. While my daughter carried on a conversation with me, she washed her little girl's food-stained face and then reached over to turn up a cuff on her dress. She pulled her over to her and adjusted her ponytail. She told her to pull her socks up and helped her tie her shoes. She patted down the wrinkles in her dress. My granddaughter took it all in stride, seeming to understand that all of this was for her own good. All of a sudden, I understood why it seems so natural for us mothers to keep telling our children what to do once they reach adulthood.

The closer we are to our children, the more opportunities we see for improvement. There are countless little things about them and how they live their lives that could use a little help. Because we have spent so many years tending to them, we remain more attuned to trivial shortcomings than anyone else will likely ever be. As I witnessed this little interchange, it was somehow reassuring to realize how naturally we come by this inclination.

We must remember, however, that that was then, and this is now. Then they accepted our control as necessary guidance. Now they see it as interference and proof that we don't accept them as they are. More than anything, now they need our respect—our appreciation and acknowledgement that they are working hard at growing up and doing a good job at that. If we point out that they need a haircut or whiter teeth or cleaner rugs, they will not only not benefit from this advice but also will likely feel hurt by our implication that they cannot manage their own lives.

■　■　■

*If we really want to help our children grow into competent adults, what they need from us most is our affirmation and stated belief in their potential.*

## Freeing Up Energy

*O*nly in the last ten years of a long life have I become aware that I do not have infinite energy. I watch in amazement as my granddaughter plays endlessly. She is the only one in her family who doesn't take a nap on Sunday afternoons. When our children were small, we dug deep into our energy reserves to keep up with them. We were chronically sleep-deprived, but we knew this was just part of motherhood. Forced to forego our own needs, we lost sight of even having any.

An advantage of having grown children is that we now have the opportunity to pay attention to our own needs for rest and recreation; however, most of us are so used to rushing around and taking care of others that we still don't tune in. How freeing it is when we learn to listen to our bodies and let the feedback we get inform our activity level.

I recently did just that: shut off the "shoulds" and listened to my body. With the Fourth of July approaching, I started thinking about the swim party and picnic I've traditionally hosted for my family. As I looked for the flag and the patriotic tablecloth, and began to plan the menu, I became aware of how exhausted I felt. I realized that I didn't want to host the party this year.

I tried valiantly to discount my needs by reminding myself, "It's only your family—it's not that big a deal. You've always done it, and they're counting on you." I even played the guilt card: "Your mother would be so disappointed." But my body continued to talk to me, and I listened. When I told my daughter of my change in plans, she didn't dissolve into tears. Instead, she said she understood and offered to host the party herself. I immediately felt lighter and freer—and more energetic.

■   ■   ■

*One of the advantages of being mothers of "adult"*
*children is that we have the freedom to match our*
*activity levels to our energy levels.*

## Change Is a Marathon, Not a Sprint

*F*airly often a client discloses her frustration about the slow pace of her personal growth. It usually sounds something like this: "When we started working together, I was amazed by the tremendous insight I gained about why I was suffering and what I needed to learn in order to live a happier life. I was so excited that I was finally finding answers. At first, I felt like I was growing by leaps and bounds. Now I'm feeling discouraged, because it seems to take forever to change any of the insights into action. I keep doing the same old things I've always done. What's wrong with me?"

I reassure my clients that there's nothing wrong with them, that this is a familiar lament. Change isn't likely to occur without insight, and insight in itself is not sufficient to shift lifelong patterns. Change requires repetition and a commitment to persevere. My job is to provide encouragement and motivation to stay the course. Even when you can picture the finish line, change is a marathon, not a sprint.

One client, a mom of a 34-year-old son, exclaimed, "Wow, I get it now. I'm creating my own misery, not to mention my son's, by having such unrealistic expectations for him and constantly trying to get him to live up to my ideas of how his life should be! I'm making myself suffer *and* making him feel bad about himself. That's huge!" She left my office that day feeling more encouraged than she had in years.

Months later, she cried and asked me, "Why am I still so hard on him? The words just keep pouring out of my mouth without my permission! It's two steps forward, one back." I explained that the simplest things to say can be the hardest to do and that the habitual grooves in her brain run deep and will take a lot of patience to reprogram.

■　■　■

*Change is not for sissies!*

## The Art of Conversation

*I* have been observing the quality of conversation I have with clients, friends and my children. I am a bit ashamed to admit that I think I have the best heart-to-hearts with my clients and my friends. I am aware of how carefully I listen to them and how supremely interested I am in what they have to say. I don't rush or lead or interrupt them. Instead, I encourage them to continue talking, giving thoughtful and kind responses—often in the form of questions—that allow them to feel comfortable enough to dig deeper and gain new perspective on their issues. I rarely give them advice.

Contrasting that high-quality contact with my dialogues with my children makes me cringe. I tend to pay less attention, ask fewer questions, sometimes interrupt, try and get them to get to the point and, though I hate to admit it, still give unsolicited advice. Since most of these conversations take place on the phone, I could blame it on the lack of face-to-face contact. But the truth is, when I talk to my clients or friends on the phone, the conversation still goes well. When talking with them, it feels as though we've been dancing together for years. With my children, I feel like I have two left feet.

The Jungian therapist, James Hillman, explains that the word "conversation" comes from two Latin words: "vertere," meaning "to turn;" and "con," meaning "with." According to him, "Conversation means to walk back and forth with someone, turning and going over the same ground" from a variety of directions until "what we already feel and think has changed into something unexpected." In that way, good conversation is a co-creation that requires concentrated focus on the present moment. It is a true art form. When it comes to my children, I see that having contact is not the same as making contact.

▪ ▪ ▪

*Good conversation is a co-creation*
*between two people who dance lightly*
*but never lose sight of where the other's feet are.*

## If They Need Us, They Won't Leave Us

*P*arenting an adult child effectively seems to have more to do with learning to let go than anything else. These lessons would have been easier to learn when our children were younger, but most of us are slow learners. Thankfully, it's never too late to learn.

When our kids were born, we had absolute control over them. In fact, they couldn't have survived without our care. After awhile, we got used to the overwhelming responsibility that accompanied that sense of power, and many of us even came to relish it. That power was seductive; it made us feel important and useful. We didn't realize then that we would lose that control when they became adults.

As older parents, deep down, many of us attempt to maintain power and control because we fear that we will lose both our hard-won identities and our importance to our kids otherwise. To avoid facing these insecurities, we use control maneuvers such as judgmental remarks, subtle signs of rejection, unsolicited advice and withdrawal of material support. Despite the fact that our strategy usually backfires, the dark truth is that being in control provides us with a safety net—if they need us, they won't leave us.

The surprising paradox is that by letting go of power and control over our adult children we are far more likely to strengthen our connection than to lose it. Although we do have to face the grief inherent in the loss of the old, achieving an adult-to-adult relationship can be very satisfying. As we deal with our empty nests and strive to respect and appreciate the adult status of our children, our need for power and control will dissipate. As my client Mary told me, "If I'd known how much stopping being a control freak would benefit my kid *and* me, I would have done it long ago."

■　■　■

*Instead of losing our children when we let go, our relationships will actually be strengthened by learning to relate to them as adults.*

## Letting Go of the Need to Be Right

*W*hen I was a child, every night at the dinner table I had to be prepared to answer the nerve-wracking question my mother, a teacher, asked: "What did you learn today?" It felt like a test. Failure was not an option, since knowing everything and being right held high premiums in my family. In fact, my parents would often challenge the facts I presented, and we'd rush to our well-worn encyclopedia to see who would win the nickel bet. I cherish the memory of the first time I proved my dad wrong—I was 11.

As a result of the underlying message I received that being wrong was not acceptable, I developed an insatiable need to be right in order to feel good about myself. I often gave my children the message that my way was the only way. The passage of years helped replace my self-righteousness with humility. While previously I had felt compelled to know everything, I began to realize that I knew a lot about a few things but very little about many others.

Parenting adult children was one area I knew very little about, and my strained relationships with my children bore this out. I was so certain about how they should be living their lives that I rarely listened for what was right for them. After years of tense and distant relations, I decided to listen more and talk less. I began to realize that sometimes I am right, and other times wrong, and that in most life decisions—hairstyles, spending patterns, parenting styles—there is no one right answer.

It seemed very strange and unnatural when I first started to tell my children, "I'm sure you'll do what you think is best." But I became accustomed to the detachment, and it was a relief not to feel responsible for their decisions. Of course I was thrilled to see their resentments toward me begin to melt away.

■   ■   ■

*Letting go of the need to be right relieves the pressure on both mothers and their adult children.*

## Letting Go of Our Need to Be Needed

*O*ne of the prevailing thoughts depressed people have is that their lives lack purpose, that their death would affect no one. Mothers of small children have a built-in protection against this devastating belief because their children need and depend on them. As the kids move toward adulthood, though, some moms hang onto their need to be needed as a hedge against feeling worthless.

My client Sally admitted to two wildly opposing thoughts as her adult son successfully completed the chemical dependency treatment she had worked so hard to get him to enter. "I'm thrilled about his accomplishment, and I'm so happy for him—he has a bright future ahead. He feels good about himself and is finally making healthy friends. But secretly I'm really afraid that, if he doesn't need me anymore, I'll lose him. The truth is that the closer he has gotten to the completion of his program, the more anxious I've felt."

Sally started to weep as she confided what, until now, had been a deep, dark secret. She admitted that, because her marriage had been rocky when her son was small, she had allied herself with her son, getting her needs for emotional intimacy met through him instead of her husband or girlfriends. Because she stayed home with her son, her life became his life, and now she faced the loss of her own emotional support.

I thanked Sally for her honesty and explained that she could help her son tremendously in his move toward independence and that she, too, would have the opportunity to do the same, since they had been mutually dependent. Through her tears, Sally told me that she loved her son enough to want to empower, rather than enslave him. She began to grasp the idea that she would help him most by letting go of her need to help.

■　■　■

*Finding other outlets of our need to be needed is the only way we can help our children become adults.*

## Re-defining Success

*P*at exposed her two young children to artistic and cultural experiences that included music and art lessons and trips to museums, concerts and ballets. She provided guidance and support so they could excel academically. She shared craft projects and played ball in the backyard. She had a clear vision of what it would take for them to succeed in the world. Well, as they say, "the best laid plans…"

When I first met Pat, a wealthy homemaker, she expressed deep disappointment when she told me, "Nothing is turning out the way it was supposed to. My daughter announced she is gay and is getting an art degree, with no intention of teaching. My son has decided to drop out of college so he can play drums in a rock band. I feel like such a failure — What did I do wrong? Don't they realize what a slap in the face this is to me? Art and music were supposed to *enhance* their lives, not *be* their lives. I wanted them to be successful."

Upon exploration, Pat discovered that her definition of success was linked to prestige and material wealth. She had been a devoted parent. Her kids were bright, curious, kind, self-confident young people. She slowly began to admit that she had expected to bask in the glory of their success, which would have, in turn, reflected her excellent parenting. Now she felt embarrassed as she anticipated telling friends and family about her kids' choices.

Pat began to search for a new definition of success. In time, she realized that both of her children seemed quite happy, and neither suffered from any addictive illness or acted irresponsibly. As she let go of her expectations for them, she began to relax into the truth that they were likely to lead happier lives than they would have if they had followed her dreams for them. We agreed that this truth suggests both success and successful parenting.

■　■　■

*After we lay the groundwork, we must trust the*
*process and allow our children to find their own way.*

## To Give or Not to Give, That Is the Question

*I*nfluenced by elders who grew up during the Great Depression, many mid-life mothers were likely born when there was relative affluence and stability. Yet the "Depression Mentality" still ruled our families. We were offered few extras beyond our basic needs for shelter, food and clothing. As a backlash, we often seem compelled to make our children's lives as comfortable as possible.

With her head down, Diana told our mothers' group that she and her husband had decided to give their young adult son a car against the advice of the treatment center from which he had recently been released. Her son learned as a young boy to pressure and manipulate his mom to get what he wanted. Diana has discovered that giving in to her son is one of the things that helps keep him sick, and yet she can't stand to see him unhappy.

Initially, Diana understood that her son was not mature enough to take good care of a vehicle. But as the weather began to worsen, she envisioned him having to walk to work in cold weather, and he began to play up that angle. Despite being confronted by everyone in our group, she began to lose her resolve. When I asked her to dig deeper to try and understand why, she began to cry as she realized that her son's discomfort reminded her of how she felt as a child when her needs were ignored.

Finally, Diana realized, "I've got to remember that I've never ignored my son's needs. Being a good mother doesn't mean giving him everything he wants. Not giving him a car comes from a place of love, not neglect. Maybe he can use those good manipulation skills to figure out how to get to work when the weather is bad."

■　■　■

*In exploring whether or not to make things easier for our children, we must discern whether our decision comes from what's right for them, or from our need to keep ourselves comfortable.*

## Grandchildren: A Second Chance

*I*t is said that grandkids are God's way of giving us a second chance. I know I'm not the only one who thinks I'm a much better grandmother than I was a mother. The wisdom that comes with life experience heightens the quality of my relationships, and the fact that I'm rarely on duty full time helps, too. But the greatest advantage is that I'm awake now: I'm conscious of the gifts and the responsibilities that come with this role.

When I became a grandma, I thought the experience would be one of pure joy, and much of it is. My heart melts when my littlest grandchild jumps up and down when she sees me. But I've been surprised to find so many growth opportunities, too. How interesting to discover that I'm dealing with some of the same issues that arose when I was raising their parents.

I told an old friend that I was feeling sad about seeing so little of my high-school grandson now. He's clearly "not that into me." She replied, "My grandkids are getting to the age that they like to be either at home or with their friends, rather than with me. The pool is somewhat of a draw, but, even when it's hot, they often opt for other activities. I know that's normal, but I guess I still want to be a big cheese in their lives." It felt good to know I'm not alone.

The difference between then and now is that today I can choose to be conscious of my feelings, accept them as valid, and share them with others who understand. I don't have to personalize this rejection or, even worse, shame my grandson for not wanting to spend time with me. Instead, I consider it a blessing that he is such a good kid that he'll visit from time to time, and I make sure I don't just sit around waiting for him to show up.

■   ■   ■

*Along with the gift of being a grandmother comes the responsibility for the growth opportunities that inevitably arise.*

## Letting Go of Knowing More

*A* recent research study concluded that relatively new physicians know more than those with many years experience. This finding goes against the prevailing wisdom equating experience with greater knowledge. The implication of the study was that patients might be better off choosing younger physicians, since they are most likely to be more up-to-date on the latest treatments.

There is an analogy here for mid-life mothers. When our children were young, there was no question that we knew more about everything than they did. It was our job to educate and illuminate them and to stimulate their curiosity. If we did a decent job with these endeavors, they went on to learn all kinds of things about which we know nothing.

Some of us hang onto the idea that we will always know more than our children. The arrogance of age suggests that the phenomenon that our children's knowledge may outgrow ours is somehow unnatural and suggests that we aren't effective role models. I remember when I attempted to help my grandson with his sixth-grade math homework. I worked very hard at trying to understand it, going back to it repeatedly, unable to accept that it was beyond my grasp.

Finally, I had to admit that I simply couldn't do it and sheepishly explained to my grandson that he would have to ask someone else. I'll never forget what he told me: "That's okay, Grammy. Nobody can know everything." As I learned from his wisdom, I was confronted by one of the most challenging aspects of parenting: my own humility.

I know that humility is good for my soul. There are still things I know that my adult kids don't know, but I have accepted and now enjoy the freedom that comes with not having to know everything. The pressure is off, and I'm free to be proud of them for how smart they are.

■　■　■

*It is not a reflection on our worth as mothers*
*to admit that our grown children*
*sometimes know more than we do.*

# · 147 ·

## Relationship Rights

*M*any times we don't like the way our relationships with our adult children feel, but we don't know exactly why. We may know what we don't like but can't really say what would feel better. We all deserve to feel respected and emotionally safe, and it really helps to have some idea of what constitutes a respectful association. The following are the some of basic relationship rights between mothers and their adult children.

- The right to have your feelings and experience acknowledged as valid and true for you.
- The right to be listened to and responded to with kindness.
- The right to present your own view, even if the other has a different view.
- The right to be free from accusation, blame and criticism.
- The right to be free from angry outbursts and rage.
- The right to a feeling of mutual respect, support and goodwill in your interactions.
- The right to receive the benefit of the doubt—an understanding that the other's best interests are at heart.
- The right to a sincere apology if the other has said or done something hurtful.

Perhaps the most important of these rights is the feeling of mutual respect, support and goodwill. If it is present, most issues can be successfully addressed because both parties know that the core intention is to honor the other's worth. As we take our own inventory, we can ask ourselves which of these we give regularly to our adult children, as well as which ones we still need to work on. It is not realistic to think we will always hit the mark on these criteria. These rights represent ideals to work toward, and it may work best if we and our children do our own assessments.

■  ■  ■

*Understanding our basic rights gives us a*
*benchmark from which to evaluate the quality of our*
*relationships with our adult children.*

## Justification

*I* watched a show that focused on meddling mothers. One participant, a 31-year-old married woman with two children, lived in a house directly behind her mother's. She asked the facilitator to help convince her mother to leave her alone. She described how her mom uses her emergency key to come in and snoop around when her daughter isn't home and then complains how she doesn't have any fresh vegetables or her floors are dirty.

The mom became defensive and stated that she was just doing what any mother who loves her children and grandchildren would do. She told the host, "I don't feel like I'm interfering. I just feel like I have lots of good advice to offer, and she should be grateful to have a mother who cares so much." Despite the audience loudly voicing their dissent, at the end of the show the mom refused to modify her behavior. The facilitator suggested that the daughter consider moving.

I was so appalled by this mother's ability to justify her abysmal behavior that I found myself yelling at the television. I heard myself say, "Lady, don't you see you're going to lose your daughter?" I felt smug and self-righteous until I suddenly remembered my first meetings with the therapist whom my daughter and I went to see in order to mend our broken relationship.

I was dismayed to recall that I had felt very much like the mom on this show. The defense mechanism of justification was so powerful that, despite my daughter's protests, I was convinced I was helping, not harming her. Slowly, I was able to see her side of the picture, but the humble pie I had to eat in order to do that sure tasted bitter. A wave of gratitude washes over me now as I realize I can no longer taste that bitterness. In fact, it has been replaced by the sweetness of a close, but respectful relationship with my precious daughter.

■　■　■

*It is freeing for us and our children when we realize*
*that there is rarely any legitimate justification for*
*interfering with their lives.*

# · 149 ·

## Change — the Only Constant

$M$any have commented on how much fun it must be for me to help people change their lives. Actually, my work is much harder than it might seem because of how resistant people are to change. They want relief from their suffering with as little required of them as possible. The scientific principle of homeostasis — that organisms always try to maintain a steady state — supports this observation. As a result, when my clients get the relief that can come after just a few sessions, they often end therapy before any lasting change can take place.

When I was going through divorce many years ago, I bought a button with a big line drawn through the word "Change." Every night, I moved the button off of that day's outfit and pinned it on the next day's outfit. I told anyone who would listen that I hated change, as though that were a novel idea. Now I realize how normal I was, but I am grateful today that I have learned to embrace change as the only constant. Today, I see mothers of adult children fighting the opportunity to evolve as parents. This resistance is understandable, given that growth requires change, which calls for hard work.

The French writer Anatole France wrote, "All changes, even the most longed for, have their melancholy; for what we leave behind us is a part of ourselves. We must die to one life before we can enter into another!" This is what we mothers have to contend with when we face our own shortcomings or our disappointment about our children, or when we must let go of our fantasies or dreams. It requires true courage to do the hard work of coming to terms with reality and taking responsibility for our own well-being. I honor each and every mother who makes the choice to do so.

■   ■   ■

*Just as we get used to yesterday, along comes today.*

## The Many Faces of Guilt

The feeling of guilt bonds all mothers together. Comedian and mother of three Erma Bombeck remarked, "Guilt is the gift that keeps on giving." While the Merriam-Webster Dictionary defines guilt as "a feeling of responsibility for offenses," I would like to amend its definition to read, "a feeling of responsibility for offenses real *and* imagined."

Guilt is our middle name, our constant companion, our state of being. Here are some of the things I've heard moms feel guilty about over the years: not spending enough quality time with their kids; not allowing them to socialize enough; having a career; not having a career; doing too much for them; not doing enough; praising them too much, or too little; keeping them involved in too many activities; not offering them enough broadening opportunities; getting divorced; and staying too long in a loveless marriage.

As parents of adult children, we have a whole new guilt inventory from which to draw: giving them too much; not supporting them enough; doing too much for them; not helping them enough; enabling their addictions; not acknowledging their strengths; and praising them so much they think they're God's gift to the world. If we work at it, we can always find ways to chastise ourselves, since chronic guilt springs from our own feelings of self-doubt and is toxic to our soul.

Guilt is a rock that sits in the bottom of our stomachs. We can learn how to evaluate what's keeping us awake at night and learn to let go of what's not helpful. If we need to apologize to our children, let us do that. If we are obsessing about things from the past, we can let them go. If we need to amend our behavior, there is nothing to stop us. But, ultimately, we must shine the brilliant light of forgiveness onto these rocks in our guts and let them melt away forever. We must learn that we aren't perfect, but we are enough.

■ ■ ■

*Chronic guilt weighs us down; learning to release it allows us to soar.*

# · 151 ·

## Learning from Our Mistakes

*I*f we are ever to free ourselves from guilt, we must become aware of our regrets and then release them. The most content mothers are not those who see themselves as infallible, but, rather, those who know they've made plenty of mistakes and have released their regrets. There is no question that all of us could have done a better job raising our children. It is the toughest job to do well, and many of us were growing up alongside our little ones.

It is not fair to blame ourselves today for what we didn't know yesterday. What *is* called for is radical acceptance of ourselves as parents. We must strive to feel deep in our hearts that we have always done the best we could with the information and resources available to us at the time. Along with a commitment to our ongoing growth, this acceptance will allow us to continue to improve as mothers. The good news is that, though we will be needed less as our children mature, we are simply moving from a full-time to a part-time job. Our services will always be needed.

With the advantage of 20-20 hindsight, we can learn to release regrets by looking for the gifts in our mistakes. Today I think back with gratitude on that horrible day when my daughter told me that, if I didn't stop interfering with her parenting, I wasn't going to be allowed to see my grandson. This announcement, very unusual for my normally agreeable daughter, was the culmination of increased tension in our relationship, and it shook me to the core of my being. That one confrontation set in motion a process of education and reflection that resulted in transformation, eventually leading me to work with many other mothers of adult children and to write this book. If that isn't a gift, I don't know what is.

■　■　■

*Good judgment comes from experience, and a lot of*
*that comes from bad judgment.*

## Ladies Who Lunch and Laugh

*T*oday I had lunch with three long-time friends. Human beings and mothers first, psychotherapists second, we are all on the journey of learning not to take ourselves too seriously. We spent hours catching up and sharing resources, but the best part of the afternoon was the abundance of guffaws we shared as we paraded out our foibles in all their glory.

Chatting away, Jane reached into her purse for a piece of paper and began to write on a panty liner. We all noticed at the same time and dissolved into gales of laughter. Later, Linda told us how, after she had completed a radio interview, she shook hands with the host of the show, and started to leave before she was suddenly jerked back into her seat by the cord, still attached to her headset. After untangling herself, she stood up again and made her exit with a sheepish grin and a shrug of her shoulders. How fun it was to share the rich word picture this story drew.

During our meal, Kathy told us she would email us information about three continuing education opportunities. When we got up to leave, she admitted that she could only remember that there were three things but had no idea what they were. Bemoaning our menopausal memory challenges, we all got a chuckle out of the fact that we, too, were at a loss. Finally, we left the restaurant, and I drove my van toward the highway. Linda called frantically from the back seat, "Wendy, you left the hatch door up!" We again laughed merrily, and I promised to pay attention and get them back home in one piece.

We all reflected on how nice it is to be able to laugh at ourselves and each other without anyone feeling offended or hurt. We agreed that the humility we have gained as a result of being mothers has helped us not to expect perfection of ourselves or others.

■  ■  ■

*It is such a relief to see the humor and accept the absurdity in everyday blunders.*

# · 153 ·

## Learning to Respect Ourselves

Stephanie came to group one night and shared excitedly, "Amanda is visiting this week, and when she was getting ready to go meet her high school friends, she asked to wear some of my jewelry." We broke into spontaneous applause and exclaimed "Congratulations!" This simple interaction was the culmination of many years of hard work on the part of a mother working to heal herself and her relationship with her young adult daughter.

Four years earlier, Stephanie's and Amanda's relationship was on the rocks, with mom feeling inferior to her daughter and Amanda reflecting back to her mother the contempt and disdain Stephanie felt toward herself. She was constantly praising her daughter, telling her how beautiful and smart she was, even as Amanda was hateful to her mom. The more she was mistreated, the harder this mom tried to please her daughter. When she started to make and sell beaded jewelry, Amanda didn't even acknowledge, let alone wear, any of the pieces her talented mom was creating.

When I met her, Stephanie didn't realize that she had any choices. She felt like a victim. Conversely, she felt empowered when she got to work on her self-esteem issues. As she learned to treat herself better, her self-perception improved, and she became unwilling to allow others to mistreat her. She stood up straighter, made clear eye contact, and combated the negative messages she had always given herself about her intelligence and competence.

Previously painfully shy, this mom attended group therapy regularly and began to climb out of her shell. She continued to admire her daughter's accomplishments, but she learned to appreciate her own, too. She spoke up to her daughter when she said something demeaning. Little by little, Amanda's treatment of her mother transformed to fondness and respect. Her asking to wear some of her mom's jewelry that evening was a concrete demonstration of the healing in their relationship. Stephanie became tearful as she realized just what this gesture meant.

■　■　■

*If we mothers learn to respect ourselves, others will respect us;*
*by changing ourselves, we can transform our relationships.*

## Motherhood Is Sisterhood

*T*he longer I work with mothers of adult children, the more I believe that we are all sisters under the skin. While our children were growing up, we spent endless hours consoling, cajoling, guiding, shopping, nursing, rocking, playing, cooking, cleaning, disciplining, waiting and driving. We were all in our own homes doing the same things: fussing over them, guiding them, delighting in them, telling them "No," cooking dinner, helping with homework and getting them off to bed.

We knew we were all in this together—even if we'd never met before, we would speak with each other in grocery stores, on soccer fields and playgrounds, often with wry smiles or rolls of the eyes, as we shared how to get fruit punch out of cotton play clothes or how we hadn't had a good night's sleep in two years. We lifted each other up, inspired each other to keep going and enjoyed the in-jokes of sisters sharing a common experience.

Now that our children are adults, that camaraderie has largely disappeared, and many mothers feel like only children. Especially when our children aren't doing as well as we or society seem to think they should, or when our parent-child relationships are strained, we keep to ourselves and think we're the only ones struggling. The truth is that now we need support just as much, and sometimes more, since their problems are more serious today than the skinned knees or bad math grades of yesterday.

It is helpful to remember that our sisterhood still exists and is filled with mothers who worry about their children, who struggle with feelings of inadequacy, who wonder how to handle situations, and who sometimes delight in their kids' sweetness, thoughtfulness or accomplishments. All it takes is reaching out to share a little with another mother to find out that we're all still in the same boat, or at least a comparable boat on the same lake.

■　■　■

*Because we are all sisters under the skin, fellowship among mothers of children of any age can comfort us.*

# · 155 ·

## Blessing in Disguise

Seven months ago, my precious daughter's massive stroke rendered her completely dependent for a time, and she has been fighting mightily to regain her independence ever since. She has suffered losses of memory, fluid speech, hearing, energy, social confidence and cognitive function, as well as the ability to sing, previously her consuming passion. After four months, she started back to work part-time but still has not resumed driving. Due to her young age, fierce determination and the countless prayers and positive thoughts of family and friends, she has made tremendous strides. We fully expect her to continue to experience subtle changes going forward.

Blessedly, I have been mostly calm during this time. Due to my own near-death experience and those of my son and granddaughter, I understand how fragile life is and that all we can really count on is today. My support group has looked after me while I've been looking after my daughter. I write regular updates to a large e-mail list, chauffeur my grandson, help my daughter stay on top of her medical concerns, and provide emotional support through daily phone calls.

During this time, I have often thought about how different things would be today if I had not done the healing work on my relationship with my daughter. Previously, she was distrustful and distant and wouldn't let me help her. She rightfully felt that I was too controlling. Today she trusts me and knows that I respect her, so she welcomes my support and help. It's as though I've been preparing for this time of need through all these years of hard work. I am humbly grateful for the opportunity to serve, and I see this experience as a true blessing in disguise. (I do wish, though, that my blessings weren't always so disguised!)

■　■　■

*We never know when or how we'll benefit from the hard work of personal growth, but we will benefit.*

## The Myth of Maturity

When we grew up, the expectation was that when we reached eighteen we would leave home. We went to college, married, joined the service, or got jobs and lived with roommates. We didn't come back. Today, if our kids leave home, they often return, sometimes with our grandchildren.

Mothers ask "Here are my grown kids still eating my food, going out every night, and changing jobs and relationships like underwear. Where did I go wrong?" Historically, children moved from adolescence right into adulthood. Today there is an intermediary stage during which young adults often live with their parents while they gain emotional and financial footing. This "boomerang" effect is a sociological trend prevalent in the United States, Europe and Asia. Twice as many 26-year-olds live with their parents today than in 1970. Some factors involved in this trend include:

1. Life is more complex today, and parents are more child-centered than ever before. Consequently, young adults expect more out of life and take longer to find themselves.

2. The previous generation's mass divorce rate has led to skepticism about marriage, so our children postpone settling down longer than ever before.

3. Young people face huge financial hurdles. A college degree is a requirement of today's job market, and enormous student loan and credit card debt, plus soaring home costs, have left young adults unable to support themselves.

Our children are a part of a profound social shift. Perhaps we should consider changing the age of maturity from 18 to 29!

■   ■   ■

*Just because our children have not yet found their way in the world doesn't mean that they won't.*

## From Caretaker to Encourager

*I*f our adult children left home and then returned, or never even moved out, we would feel confused and confounded about how to relate to them. It is clear they still need us, but in a different way than they did earlier in their lives. As they are traversing the rocky path toward emotional and financial independence, we must also travel along a parallel path that will take us from being caretakers to encouragers, from parents to mentors. That transition can be just as hard for us as the road to independence is for our children.

In years past, our job duties included fixing our kids' problems, exposing them to the best opportunities possible, and softening the harsh consequences of their immature behavior. But now we must take up a more collaborative role, and our parenting might include all of the following: sharing our experience and knowledge (if they'll let us); expressing our confidence in their bright futures; and allowing them to deal with the consequences of their own behaviors.

Terry Hargrave, a professor of counseling at West Texas A & M University, believes that the new model of the modern family with adult children still living with their parents should be one of responsible adult roommates working together toward resolving problems and accomplishing goals. He stresses the importance of the twin goals of independence for the adult child and supportive collaboration without emotional over-involvement for the parents.

Most of us had a view of our still-at-home children as lazy or of ourselves as failures. If we shift our perception to one in which we see our children as tasting the pleasures of responsibility, searching for their true identities, and pursuing their life paths, we can then view ourselves as the encouragers of these worthy endeavors and free ourselves of chronic resentment toward us and them.

■　■　■

*A paradigm shift that allows us to see our emerging adult children as being on the road to somewhere instead of nowhere can free us to encourage this important rite of passage.*

## Boundaries for Boomerang Kids

We understand that our children may take longer today to be ready to be on their own. If we have kindly agreed to allow them to live with us for awhile, we can support them in the direction of independence. In order to not feel like martyrs, it is essential that we develop and agree upon clear guidelines and the consequences if these are not met. That way, our kids know where they stand, and we can step aside and allow them to find their own way.

For example, a mother I worked with had a son who stayed out on his own after college, but couldn't make ends meet with his low-paying job and asked to move back home for a time. They had several honest discussions about how to make this work, and all guidelines were written down and signed by all parties. Her son agreed to work full-time while in graduate school and to pay his mom a small monthly rent payment and a percentage of the utility bills. He would also save monthly an amount equal to twice what he would pay his mom, and they agreed that his stay would last no longer than two years.

This wise mom agreed not to impose any curfews, but asked her son to let her know if he would be staying out overnight. She consented to keeping his bedroom door closed as long as he helped keep the common areas clean. Each would be responsible for their own laundry and meal preparation, although this mom loved to try out new recipes on her son. If there were any major violations of their arrangement, her son would have one month to move out. When he finished his graduate program, her son got a better-paying job and was able to move out in just under two years. By this time, their relationship was better than ever.

■　■　■

*With thorough preparation and accountability,*
*having our adult children live with us can be enriching*
*for everyone.*

## How Do I Love Thee? Let Me Count the Cars!

*A*common complaint I hear from mothers of adult children is the way in which they feel they "have to" keep shelling out money for their children's vehicles. They receive frantic phone calls as their kids wait alongside the road, stranded by their broken-down cars. The parents jump on their white horses and call emergency vehicle assistance as they gallop down the street to rescue their progeny. Then, because their children have no savings and are barely paying their rent, they ask for "a loan – just until payday," since they can't imagine a day without a car. The loan never gets repaid, and the accounts receivable, along with the accompanying worries and resentments, mount up.

Anne estimates that she and her husband have purchased four cars for their 30-year-old daughter and paid to fix her disabled vehicles at least 20 times. Her rationale: "If we don't help her, she won't be able to get to work, and she'll get fired. Then she won't pay her rent, and she'll get evicted. Then she'll have to move back in with us. This is the only way we can keep her out of our house."

Fiscal irresponsibility was nothing new for Anne's daughter. She had never paid her parents back one dime, and this mom admitted she had never set any limits on her willingness to rescue her daughter, who had clearly come to expect the bailout. Anne eventually saw the flaw in her rationale: she and her husband didn't need to keep their daughter's car running to prevent her from moving back in with them. They were in control of that decision, and they realized they could simply tell her, "No."

At first she felt as though she were abandoning her daughter as she began to set limits on the aid she offered. But, in time, Anne was amazed to see her daughter developing the ability to handle her own problems, both vehicle and otherwise.

■ ■ ■

*The problems our children create are their responsibility; we have enough trouble with our own.*

## When Is the Right Time to Move Out?

*T*oday, even armed with college degrees, our adult children often don't make enough money upon graduation to be financially independent. They are also still searching for who they are and are often ill-prepared for the real world. So they move back in with their parents, who then wonder when the time will be right for them to move out on their own. Sometimes the question gets answered for them.

By the time Drew found out that there were no jobs open to him at the bachelor's level, it was too late to change his major. So, with no money for graduate school and degree in hand, he returned to his mom Meg's house and began to work at a satisfying, though poorly-paying, job with no benefits.

The contract was that his mom would pay his expenses so that he could save his earnings. He was a good roommate, and Meg enjoyed his company. Drew spent most of his free time with his friends and girlfriend. Two years later, he decided that it was time for him to be on his own. He found a sales job and immediately made twice as much as he had previously. He and two friends rented an apartment and prepared to move in together.

Meg asked if he didn't think he should save money first, but a wiser, more mature Drew told her, "Mom, I've got to try this now. I love being here with you, but you make things too easy for me. I've hardly saved any money, and I haven't learned to cook or clean, either. I don't even know what things cost. If I stay here, I'll never grow up." Meg knew he was right and, after he promised to come for dinner on Sundays, she proudly and sadly sent him on his way. They both knew that, although it may not have been the perfect time, it was the right time.

■　■　■

*Our children don't have to be fully prepared for all potential pitfalls in order to be ready to be on their own.*

## Worrying Is Normal, but Not Healthy

*L*ast week I saw three mothers who share a belief that worrying about their adult children is mandatory. Joy, a 60-year-old mother, asked what I would be doing during my vacation. When I told her about my book and its subject matter, she answered breezily, "You should talk to my three kids—they all think I worry way too much. But I tell them that's just what mothers do."

Carmen, a 74-year-old mother of two, was referred to therapy by her sons and doctor. She seemed to think she was doing fine. Her doctor and sons all disagreed, describing Carmen as highly anxious, constantly worrying about her health, sons and their families. She was shocked when I shared their impressions with her. "This is just the way I am. I've always been a worrywart. Isn't every mother?" she asked me.

Susan, 39, was preparing to send her child off to college and told me that her husband had called her a "nervous wreck" about their daughter Emily, who is "the greatest kid ever"—on full scholarship, doesn't drink or do drugs, "and yet I've been having this recurring dream about her being on that big campus and not being able to find her way to classes or her dorm. I just want to climb into her suitcase and go with her."

All of these moms were oblivious to the adverse effects of their obsessive thoughts. We mothers have been fretting about our kids for so long that worrying is considered synonymous with love. Therefore, it is a revolutionary idea that, although it may be normal, worrying is a symptom of anxiety and can take a terrible toll on our health and well-being. We can learn to let go of things over which we have no control and to use self-soothing techniques to calm ourselves. But first we have to recognize and accept that worrying is a problem that was learned and can be unlearned.

■ ■ ■

*Caring about our adult children is essential;*
*worrying about them is optional.*

## Pat on the Back

*I* believe that becoming a mother is one of the best ways to grow up and beyond our feelings of self-importance. There is something inherently humbling about poopy diapers, snotty noses and ugly artwork on the refrigerator. Billy Collins, once the Poet Laureate of the United States, wrote a hilarious but touching poem about mother's love in which he recalled being a young boy at summer camp, where he learned to braid thin plastic strips into a lanyard. Even then, he knew he was creating a useless and worthless object, but it was his gift to his mother. Even though he had never seen anyone use a lanyard, he kept crossing strand over strand until he'd finished.

The body of the poem consists of Collins comparing his gift to what his mother did for him and always coming up absurdly short. He reflects on how his mother gave him life and milk from her breast, and he gave her a lanyard; how she saw him through countless illnesses, with many a sleepless night, and he gave her a lanyard; how she taught him to walk and swim, and cooked him thousands of meals, and gave him clothing and a good education, and all he could come up with for her was a lanyard.

The poem's ending speaks to the poignant truth that our love is so boundless that it transcends the obvious imbalance and makes the uneven exchange between mother and child somehow even. Children can't repay their mothers because mothers don't expect repayment. So, let's give ourselves a collective pat on the back and breathe in the affirmation that we have loved our children not perfectly, but deeply and well, and that love, freely given, is its own reward.

■　■　■

*No matter how imperfect we may have been as
mothers, let us rest in the knowledge that our effort
will always beat out the lanyard we got in return.*

# · 163 ·

## The *Experience* of Change

*M*any of us were convinced that we were going to be very different from our mothers. We determined to do better in whatever ways we felt wounded. Although we found this endeavor to be much easier said than done, it is never too late to create a climate of change. Research shows that it can take up to three generations for family members to free themselves from a familial pattern. We are all members of a tribe that preceded us. We responded to our own children based on our family of origin's responses to us. It is a "hand-me-down" system with a life of its own.

We can not think our way out of our usual manner of doing things; we must *experience* something different that challenges our old belief systems and ways of coping with the world. By being willing to challenge the status quo and by taking risks, we can then create an environment of new feelings, thoughts, beliefs and actions. When we *experience* something different inside, then our life as we know it will come to an end, and small steps will in time result in transformation.

Joan, a mother of three grown children, realized how sad she felt that her mother had never told her she loved her. She lamented that, except on birthday cards, she had never told her children either. Her internal *experience* of sadness led her to create a new experience that resulted in different feelings and actions. Although at first it felt unnatural and uncomfortable, she began telling her mom and kids "I love you" at the end of all conversations. Little by little, as they began to reciprocate, she felt the generational walls of coldness crumble.

■　■　■

*When we create an environment for the* experience *of change, life as we know it will never be the same.*

## Slow Down and Smell Those Roses

Scientist H.G. Wells said, "We must not allow the clock and the calendar to blind us to the fact that each moment of life is a miracle and a mystery." Today most of us hurry through our days, rarely taking time to smell even one rose. One study indicates that, by doing things simultaneously, we are crowding 31 hours of activity into a 24-hour-day. A recent study found multi-tasking to be more time-consuming and tiring for the brain than performing one task at a time, with resulting symptoms including fatigue, short-term memory loss and an increase in stress hormones, which cause us to feel on edge.

The antidote to multi-tasking is to learn to stay present and focus on completing one thing at a time. Here are some steps we can take in our quest for more balance.

- Take your time. Sometimes we rush out of habit instead of need. We can choose to slow down and be more mindful, which slows our heart rate, quashes that rushed feeling and engages our senses. We can smell the rain coming, hear the birds chirping or taste the soup.

- Set priorities. Our stress often stems from the "list" we've created. We can reflect on what is really essential and what can be put off, using an A-B-C system, with the A's being the most important. We can even be choosy about what makes the list, learn to say "No," and delegate whenever possible.

- Lower your standards. At the end of our lives, no one is going to say, "She didn't clean her house every week," or "She should have worked more." What really matters are making a difference and nurturing our relationships. J.K. Rowling put her housework on hiatus for the four years she was working on the Harry Potter series. When we focus on what really matters, we feel more at peace.

■　■　■

*In the pursuit of a balanced and meaningful life,*
*less is more.*

# The Need to "Improve" Our Daughters

*I*n her book, *You're Wearing That? Understanding Mothers and Daughters in Conversation*, author Deborah Tannen details the complicated connection between mothers and daughters because of how important we are to each other. A remark coming from one to the other can be either more healing or more hurtful than the same remark coming from anyone else. In her interviews, the complaint this author heard most often from grown daughters was, "She's always criticizing me." And one of the Big Three topics about which mothers tended to criticize most was their daughters' weight. (The other two were hair and clothing).

It is summer as I write this entry. Just this week three of my clients, lovely young women in their 30s, returned from trips to visit their families. They all reported that, almost immediately upon arrival, their mothers commented on their weight. One mother's first words to her daughter as she stepped out of the jet way were, "Wow, you've packed on a quite a few pounds, haven't you?" Another's mother and grandmother were so relentless at trying to manage what she ate that she cut short her visit by a few days.

All daughters want to feel that their mothers approve of them. And yet, with our society's obsession with youth and body image, coupled with the pressure to raise perfect children, it is normal for mothers to see room for improvement in their daughters. We tend to see them as reflections of us, so that if they have a weight (or hair, or clothing) problem, we believe this issue points out our imperfections and feel compelled to correct our wrong. Even the most offhand comment can sting like the biggest bee. So if we ask, "Are you sure you need that piece of cake tonight, dear?" our daughters will accurately perceive our words as criticism, the opposite of approval.

■ ■ ■

*Because we know how important our impressions of our daughters are to them, we choose to keep to ourselves any ideas we may have about how to improve them.*

## He's Baaack!

*S*andy came to therapy because of the chronic tension in her relationship with her 19-year-old son. Their power struggle was maintained by Ben's efforts to break away and hers to hold on. As I helped Sandy transition being a parent of a young adult, their relationship gradually improved. One year later, with his parents' blessing, Ben moved into an apartment with his girlfriend. Sandy filled her empty nest with church and craft projects and learned to stop worrying.

Their emotional connection intact, Ben soon confided in his mom that he was having a rough time. He felt pressured by his girlfriend to spend more time with her, while having trouble finding the time to study while working the 50 hours a week necessary to make ends meet. He was worrying a lot and having trouble sleeping. Since Sandy had learned to listen with empathy and without giving advice, she was able to comfort her son.

Eighteen months later, Sandy and her husband received a call from Ben, who tearfully announced that his relationship had ended. He felt like a failure because he hadn't been able to handle being on his own and asked if he could move back home until he finished college. They told him that they were proud of him for trying to make it work and equally proud about him knowing when he needed help. Within a week, he had moved back in.

Upon her return to therapy, Sandy's first words were "He's baaack!" I knew just what she meant. This time our work focused on setting up appropriate financial and other boundaries for Ben. She expressed gratitude that she understood how normal it is for young adults today to need more support from their parents than in previous generations. She felt confident about returning to her role of hands-on mom, but, in order to assure that she wouldn't lose herself, Sandy committed to continuing her volunteer and craft projects and returning for monthly therapy sessions.

■　■　■

***Becoming a confident and effective mother of adult children requires a set of skills that can be learned.***

# · 167 ·

## The Joy of Giving

*R*ecently I attended my little granddaughter Sheryl's family birthday party. We arrived at her favorite restaurant loaded down with presents festively wrapped in balloon paper and her favorite chocolate cupcakes. She was dressed in the lavender dress I had bought her, with hair ribbons holding back her wavy blond hair. I was aware of how excited I was to have her open the presents I had bought for her and made sure I had the extra camera batteries for my camera so I could capture the joy of the moment.

Many people stopped by our table to comment on her bounty and to wish her a happy day, and Sheryl beamed as she began opening her gifts. Lots of ooohing and ahhhing and cameras flashing added to the excitement. Sheryl loved everything I gave her and gave me a spontaneous hug after she opened her fake plastic food and miniature dinnerware, a brilliant choice for a child who aspires to be a waitress!

Mentioning to her dad that I had bought her more than I had planned, he agreed that they had done the same. "She's easy to spoil," he told me. Feeling the warmth of deep satisfaction reminded me of how much fun it is to make people happy. I couldn't help but reflect on how seeing our kids' and grandkids' faces light up when we give them gifts is a peak mothering experience.

Now I have a clearer understanding of why it is so hard for us mothers not to give our adult children everything they want or need. It's normal to want to bring a smile to the faces of those we love. Conversely, we hurt when they hurt and feel even worse when we know we could erase their distress. It helps me to remember that what made Sheryl's birthday party so special was that it only happens once a year.

■　■　■

*Giving money or material gifts to our adult children remains special only if it is out of the ordinary.*

## Releasing the Guilt from Divorce

*W*e mothers tend to feel guilty about putting our children through divorce and worry that this experience has much to do with their adult children's struggles. Since continuing to feel responsible for our offspring's troubles is never productive, we must find ways to forgive ourselves. In order to heal, we must be able to look at the benefits that came from our divorces, at the strengths our children developed as a result of that turmoil, and at what we *did* do right. Suzanne gave me permission to share the writing which she used to help release herself from the guilt of marrying, and later divorcing, her alcoholic husband.

"I wasn't able to give my sons a father who looked forward to coming into the home after a full day of work and spending the evening offering them his undivided attention, spiritual leadership, emotional safety.

"I wasn't able to give my sons a look at a mom and dad who were committed to each other in love and devotion, stood together as a team, and modeled appropriate and obvious affection for each other.

"I wasn't able to give my sons a peaceful and safe haven, where they could live unafraid to be themselves, where there was frequent laughter and few tears, where they could bring their friends home to play.

"When I got divorced, however, I freed my sons and me from the threat of yelling and being ridiculed, and I put our family back together. Though I wasn't able to give them a palace, I did create a safe refuge from their father and the cold, cruel world. I know that we were better off then.

"What I did give my sons was someone who would listen and love them well. I gave them chances to learn from my mistakes, to develop resiliency and the ability to handle strife. I gave them the best I knew and all I could. I pray it has been enough."

■　■　■

*We can choose to be kind and gentle and to forgive
ourselves for our marriages not working out.*

## I Am Me and You Are You

*J*ulie arrived for Mothers' Group excited to share her latest triumph. "More and more I get it that what's going on with my kids isn't what upsets me; it's my *reaction* to what's going on that makes or breaks my peace of mind," she told me. According to Julie, her daughter Emily is "a world class drama queen" who has often succeeded in ruining family gatherings. But Julie has been working hard on strengthening her emotional boundaries so that she can resist being drawn into the drama.

This mom described a party she had planned for her two daughters' husbands, who shared the same birthday week. She had cooked favorite foods, wrapped presents, blown up balloons, and prepared several party games she knew all would enjoy. As soon as Emily arrived, her mom knew another calamity was brewing. Face blotchy and tear-stained, her daughter handed her mom a few presents and told her tearfully, "These are for Tim—Wish him a happy birthday. We won't be staying." Her son-in-law looked apologetic and shrugged his shoulders, and they walked back down the driveway and drove away.

"The miracle," Julie described, "is that I simply returned to the family room, gave Tim his presents, and explained that Emily and Jim had dropped off the gifts, but wouldn't be staying. In the past, I would have been a wreck, feeling worried and calling her to see if they would come back. Then she would tell me the whole story, often with him yelling in the background, and I would get drawn into it all and then not know how to get out. But today I felt absolutely no desire to call her, and we went on and had a very nice party. For the first time, my boundaries were strong enough that I didn't let Emily's misery become mine and ruin my evening. I held onto myself. I can't believe how good that felt."

■　■　■

*We can't fix our adult children's problems, but* **we can**
*learn that their problems aren't* **ours.**

## Observing from the Sidelines

*D*uring a family dinner, I observed my adolescent grandson try to convince his mom that he should be able to go over to spend the evening with his girlfriend. When this discussion began, I immediately recognized their familiar dynamic. The difference this time was that I chose to stay out of it and, instead, watched the exchange from a distance. It was as though I were sitting on the bench at a tennis match between two players I barely knew, rather than two players in desperate need of a coach. I saw my daughter continually underestimate my grandson's tenacity as she tried to convince him that her reasons were compelling and sufficient.

My grandson explained that, despite the fact that she had thrown up several times that morning and had just started on antibiotics, his girlfriend was feeling better tonight and hoped he would come over to keep her company. My daughter countered with various explanations of why she didn't want him to go, including his failure to approach her with a concrete plan ahead of time, his girlfriend needing time to rest and let her medicine kick in, and complications with transportation. This bantering and bartering went on for nearly fifteen minutes while I sat there dispassionately, watching the proceedings and reflecting on what I would have done in the past.

Previously, I would not have been able to stand the length of this interchange and would have felt compelled to enter into the fray, sometimes standing behind my daughter, and, at other times, my grandson. I might have coached my daughter on how to be firmer and extricate herself from the debate, or I might have given my grandson a more compelling piece of ammunition to use in his fight for whatever he wanted. This time, I remembered that I was there not as coach or therapist, but as mom and grandma, and I just sat back and enjoyed the show.

■　■　■

*Maybe it's what we don't say to our adult children*
*that saves us.*

## Hard Work Pays Off

*I*t is exceedingly hard work to become conscious of what we say and how we act around our adult children. But the changes that take place when we stop interfering and learn to be respectful really pay off in improved trust, clearer communication and increased warmth. Even though we'll never be perfect, any work we do can make a difference.

Sally told me of a small triumph that occurred as she stopped trying to control her only child. In the past, she had criticized Jackie's weight, clothes and hair; choice of boyfriends; the messiness of her apartment; and nearly every aspect of her daughter's life except her career as an attorney. Even then, although proud of her daughter's accomplishments, Sally still wanted to control where she worked and how much money she made.

When they began working on their relationship, Jackie was seriously considering severing all ties with her mom. At first, this mom was quite defensive, and Jackie was equally intolerant. But, in time, Sally began to be able to stop and listen to how hurtful her constant disapproval was to her daughter, and she started containing her compulsion to control. Jackie became more understanding as she saw how hard her mom was working, and gradually they were able to have a conversation in which each listened to the other and provided empathy and support, rather than advice and censure.

Finally, Jackie agreed to accompany her family on a week-long camping trip. When Sally returned, she told me that she had become ill on the trip and had regressed to her old habit of picking on her daughter. When she felt better, she was able to apologize to Jackie and was very pleased to hear a compassionate response from her daughter, who said, "That's okay, Mom — I knew you weren't feeling well, and I knew you didn't really mean what you were saying."

■　■　■

*When we take responsibility for the quality of our relationships, our adult children will likely reward us by cutting us slack when we backslide.*

## Mothers are Daughters, too

*D*uring a recent lunch with an old girlfriend, I was reminded that we mothers are daughters, too. Linda, 55 years old and the mother of two, recounted an unpleasant phone conversation she had just had with her mother. Due to chronic criticism and disapproval, my attractive and personable friend's relationship with her mom has always been strained. Although Linda is certain that her mom's inability to appreciate and affirm her stems from an outward projection of her mom's low self esteem, the barbs from her words still sting my dear friend.

"I just called to tell her I was thinking of her because I'll be canning peaches this weekend. We used to have fun doing that together, and I thought it would be fun to share in the memory. I just hoped that maybe we could keep the conversation light and pleasant for once. But nooooo, my mom would never miss a chance to say something mean," she explained. Linda then related that, when she said she needed to get off the phone so she could go to her hair appointment, her mother responded, "Linda, you really need to do something about that hair. It is way too short, and it isn't very becoming, especially now that you aren't so young anymore."

Although she has learned a lot about how not to take on her mom's criticism seriously, Linda still felt deflated and disheartened when we met. I was struck by how important it is that we women be able to share our emotional pain with others who understand. "I'm so glad we can talk, because I know you get it. It wasn't like I was shocked by what my mom said," she told me, "It was just that I was hoping that we could just get through one conversation without her shaming me. The good news is that I am even more aware of the cautionary tale here: I will *not* do the same thing to my kids. This pattern *will* end with me."

■　■　■

*The benefits of short, pleasant conversation with our adult children cannot be overestimated.*

## Mirth is Good Medicine

*I*t's important to remember that we, and only we, have responsibility for the quality of our everyday lives. Although we have spent our lives tending to the care and feeding of our children, one of the perks of letting them go is that now we have more time to tune into what creates balance and joy for us. Dr. Lee Berk of the Center for Neuroimmunology at Loma Linda University Medical Center, has for many years been a leading authority on the effects of laughter on our immune system, which regulates our health. In his work, he distinguishes between "mirthful," meaning "happy," and "coping," meaning "black" humor, since they each have different results on the immune system.

To study the effects of "mirthful laughter," Dr. Berk's team took blood samples from their subjects before, during and after they watched funny videos. His research showed that, without question, mirthful laughter increased the number of T-cells with helper markers. These cells, also known as "happy cells," divided and spread in a way that helped them regulate the immune response that keeps us well. Dr. Berk did not find similar results with dark humor, in which someone else was the butt of the jokes.

Intuitively, I know that I must balance the seriousness of my work with light and laughter. I love to watch funny but sweet movies. I am on a regular "news diet," which means I keep myself informed while restricting my access to news stories. I have never seen many of the great films of modern times, including "Titanic," "Schindler's List," or "The Hurt Locker" because there is too much tragedy and violence.

And I make sure that I watch something that makes me laugh every day. My favorite television show is "The Ellen DeGeneres Show," since she never fails to produce mirthful laughter with her cheerful, kind and hilarious observations of the human experience. I record her show on DVR, and, late at night, I can be found in my living room, laughing out loud right along with Ellen.

■　■　■

*Mirthful laughter is good medicine for whatever ails us.*

## Worrying is a Cultural Trend

*O*ur parents worried much less about us than we worry about our children. Their focus emphasized education and financial independence. In contrast, today's parents are the first generation for whom our children's emotional fulfillment is a primary goal. Feeling responsible for our children's happiness is only one factor contributing to today's parents increased worrying. Some other factors:

1. Parents wait longer to have children and then have smaller families, with increased focus on the needs of their individual children.

2. We tend to correct for the lack of emotional attachment between our parents and ourselves by overindulging our children.

3. We feel increased guilt because of so many more mothers in the workplace and the much higher divorce rate.

4. With five times more parenting books available today than in 1970, we read too much and then feel inadequate.

5. The media hypes all the things that can go wrong in our children's lives.

6. The financial picture has changed dramatically, leading to the high cost of housing, increased need for college degrees and an unstable job market.

Parents used to believe their job was done when their children reached age 18. Because societal perception of when adulthood begins has now changed to the middle to late 20s, our sense of responsibility lingers. Perhaps looking for some middle ground between these two extremes could free us from the tyranny of society's perfectionism and our resultant worrying. Perhaps we could learn to say, "Good enough."

■　■　■

*Since worry reveals as much about us as parents*
*as it does about our children,*
*it pays for us to look in the mirror.*

## The Elusive Middle Ground

We are a nation of extremists. We like to reduce things to simplistic concepts so that we can feel more comfortable. We tend to think in terms of all or nothing, black or white, always or never, right or wrong. We forget that, between each of these poles, there is an enormous area of unexplored territory well worth investigating. We mothers often go to extremes, too, sometimes in an attempt to offset the way we were treated as children.

For example, in my family of origin, we never talked about sexuality. Even witnessing a couple kissing on a television program was excruciatingly embarrassing for all of us. When I became a mother, I was determined to eliminate this repression, and I kept my commitment to a fault. In a misguided attempt to help my children feel comfortable with their own bodies, I often went without clothes at home. Instead of teaching the value of privacy and healthy sexuality, I went from having walls to having almost no boundaries. I didn't know any better then, but now I do.

Now I understand that the vast wilderness between the poles of A and Z is well worth exploring, because there are many viable actions hidden within their depths. When making decisions about how to handle situations with our adult children, it pays to remember that, although our default mode may be to gravitate toward extremes, we can resist this temptation and examine the middle ground. We can strive to exhibit healthy boundaries, rather than either no boundaries or rigid walls. In this way, our choices will be life-affirming to ourselves and our kids.

For example, if my son does something hurtful to me, rather than choosing the extremes of either pretending it didn't happen or of blasting him, I can step back, collect my thoughts and feelings, and then either let it go or talk with him in an appropriate manner.

▪ ▪ ▪

*With all the choices available between the extremes of A and Z, we can explore and perhaps strive for somewhere between J and P.*

## Are You a "Someday" Person?

When our children were small, any dreams that we had for us had to be put on hold while we focused our energies on raising our children. We got so good at sacrificing, putting out fires, and keeping our kids in soccer and underwear that our own dreams got tucked into the deep recesses of the file marked "Someday." Maybe these aspirations were of places we wanted to visit, or perhaps career paths or hobbies we wanted to explore. Today, as we have more time to live our own lives, we have the chance to dust off that old file and look inside again.

We may be surprised to find this endeavor is easier said than done, however. We got into such a habit of thinking in terms of "Someday" that we may still operate that way, even if our children are launched. The fact is that it can be scary to face our deepest heart's desires, for then we face the risk of disappointment or failure. It's easier, though not as satisfying, to maintain the status quo and convince ourselves that we're happy just as we are. The eminent philosopher Carl Jung once said, "Your vision will become clear only when you look into your heart. Who looks outside, dreams. Who looks inside, awakens."

We mothers can dare to peek inside our hearts, to catch a glimpse of something which will make our hearts sing. It took me years after my kids were out on their own to give myself permission to play again. Taking piano lessons after 40 years away, learning to create memory books, and even writing this book have brought me pure joy. You may want to learn to paint with acrylics, plan that long-yearned-for trip to Ireland, or even explore an entirely new career. It never hurts to dream. When attached to action, dreams do come true.

■　■　■

*Larry McMurtrey, the folksy author of Lonesome Dove, cuts to the chase when he says, "If you wait, all that happens is that you get older. Don't wait."*

## Is Your Cup Half Empty or Half Full?

*T*he members of my family have exceedingly high, and often unrealistic, expectations for themselves and others. Most in my extended family have advanced college degrees and are successful professionals. There is a high premium placed on stoicism and perfection, and not a lot of room for vulnerability, neediness or stumbling around trying to find your place in the world. There is little acceptance of impairment or inadequacy in any area, whether it be emotional, relational, financial or intellectual. The driven quality of their lives keeps some members from being deeply satisfied with their lives.

Although hard to admit, I am a member of this family. For many years, I played by its rules, worshipping a few and feeling disappointed by all others, including my adult children. I desperately chased after the flawlessness that was always out of reach. Because I either felt better or worse than others, I always felt the pain and loneliness of separation. I would gaze at the cup that represented my life, and that cup always seemed half-empty.

Today I am more content. As I continue to release my family's inhuman goals, my relationships have improved. Now I understand how soul-draining and negative this "half-empty" way of relating to self and others is, and how freeing it feels to cut others slack. I have brought my expectations in line with the reality that we are all imperfect, making mistakes every day and doing about the best we can, given the baggage we're all lugging around.

My daily goal is to be kind and compassionate to myself, my children and others. Because I'm human, I don't always succeed, but that doesn't keep me from trying. Today I strive for excellence, not perfection, and I have transformed my perception of that cup. While my cup contains the same people and the same mixture of heartbreak and joy, now it nearly always seems well more than half full.

■ ■ ■

*Compassion becomes real when we recognize our shared humanity.*

## Life Is Messy

*J*ackie started crying as soon as we began our session. She told me about the complications related to her daughter's upcoming wedding. Her son was not going to make it home from the service overseas in time for the rehearsal dinner and maybe not even for the ceremony. Her daughter's future mother-in-law was insisting on adding names to the guest list two weeks after the deadline for RSVPs, and the photographer, a friend who had offered to take the pictures as his wedding gift, had just been admitted to drug rehab and wouldn't complete his program until after the wedding. "Why don't things ever turn out the way they're supposed to?" Jackie murmured through her tears.

"'The way they're supposed to' according to whom?" I asked gently. Jackie stopped to ponder this question as though I were asking about the meaning of life, which, perhaps, in a way, I was. She told me, "I guess I just always thought that, if I was a good person and treated people well, things would just fall into place. Instead, it seems like my life is always in chaos. I'm exhausted and just wonder when things will settle down. I always had this dream of my daughter's fairytale wedding, and, instead, the dream has turned into a nightmare."

I reassured Jackie that weddings are always stressful, but that things do get resolved, and her daughter would have her magical day, though perhaps not exactly the day this mom had envisioned. But then I explained the larger issue: Life is messy. We have very little control over anyone but ourselves, and it is normal for things not to turn out as we might wish. As Rabbi Harold Kushner told us, "Bad things happen to good people." When we learn to embrace the messiness of life, instead of expecting everything to be tied up in nice, neat packages, then we aren't always frustrated and disappointed and can, instead, see life as a glorious adventure.

■ ■ ■

***Bless this mess.***

## Everyone's Nest Empties Differently

*M*ost people seem to believe that mothers have one of two basic reactions to an upcoming empty nest: Busy career women with full lives are expected to barely notice their children's departure, while stay-at-home moms, who have devoted their lives to the care of their kids, are expected to sink into deep despair. I have found that moms' reactions are impossible to predict, and every reaction is valid.

One mother I know, a busy attorney, expected to breeze right through taking her daughter to college. "It was such a shock when the grief came out of left field and hit me hard. I started crying before she left, and I cried after she was gone. Every day I worried about her. Would she make friends? Would her clothes be all right? Would she be able to handle the schoolwork? And I missed her, especially every morning, when we had our little routine of eating breakfast and talking about our days. I was kind of embarrassed, thinking I should be stronger. It is a huge relief to know that mine was a perfectly normal reaction," this mom said.

Another mom, who stopped teaching right before she married and poured her entire life into the care of her family, was equally surprised when her youngest child was preparing to leave home to join the Marine Corps. "Everyone told me that I should prepare myself for a major grief reaction," she said, "So I was on the lookout for tears and depression, even being aware of our 'last times' together, like 'Oh, this is the last time I'll go with him to the dentist.' I was a little sad when we put him on the plane, but my predominant feeling was relief that now all my kids are launched, and I can focus on my own dreams at last. When my friends called to see how I was doing, I was almost embarrassed to tell them how excited I was about my plans to go back to school."

▪ ▪ ▪

*Our feelings are our own unique expression of our experiences; whatever we feel is valid for us.*

## Is It Grief or Depression?

*M*ost mothers of adult children are on a first-name basis with grief. We mourn and feel empty when our children leave home, or we feel sorrow about our lost freedom if they return home. There are many other, more existential, occasions that can leave us heartbroken, too, including the loss of our dreams if our children tell us they are gay, or have decided to move far away or not to have children.

It is important that we both give ourselves permission to grieve and learn to distinguish grief from depression. Well-meaning people often don't know how to handle our raw emotions. They may say things like, "Now everybody's children leave home. He'll be back at Thanksgiving." Or "You should be proud of her—At least she didn't bring unwanted kids into the world." These types of comments can cause us to feel guilty or embarrassed about what's natural, which can lead to repression and then depression or emotion-related illnesses such as irritable bowel syndrome or headaches.

In our society, reliance on intellect at the expense of feelings is an epidemic. Most people are uncomfortable with uncomfortable feelings. Physicians want to medicate their patients' grief. We are told, "Don't cry; be strong; don't feel bad," instead of honoring grief as an organic process built into us as the most natural way of letting go of something or someone important to us.

Grief, though often raw, has an honest, almost pure feel to it, and it has movement. It does not include the self-hatred, isolation, or stuck feelings that go along with most depression. Grief has fluidity, comes in waves, and most grieving people can go about their daily lives. If allowed to unfold, grief will, in time, resolve. Untreated depression, on the other hand, tends to stay the same, or even get worse over time. Tissues, not tranquilizers, are the way through grief.

■　■　■

*The grief experience is a natural process that should always be honored.*

## Learning from Our Children

*M*y son loves to surf. When he was a little boy, he spent every minute he wasn't in school on a skateboard or a bike. When he moved near the ocean, he made the easy transition to a surfboard. Since then, he has also taken up snowboarding, but surfing remains his passion—He even took a surfing vacation to Costa Rica. I used to be baffled by his desire to spend his free time lying in the ocean on his board. It seemed to me to be a monumental waste of time, since he might only find five or six waves each day that he considered worth riding. And yet, there he was, every weekend. When his son got old enough, he was there with him.

Mystified as to why my son, a high achieving young man chasing the American dream, spent year after year on that board, one day I asked him about the obvious appeal surfing has for him and for countless others who don't fit the laid back, hang-ten surfer stereotype. "It keeps me sane and balances me, Mom," he told me. "It helps me slow down after my hectic week. It's my meditation."

"Surfing teaches me to live in the moment and be patient," he continued. "I'm there to be at one with the board and the water, not to see how many great waves I can catch. Don't get me wrong—it's awesome to catch a big one, but I'm not all tense waiting for it. Surfing reminds me that nature has its own rhythm, and that I'm a part of nature. So it helps me pay attention to my own rhythm, too. Believe it or not, it makes me a better person and helps me stay in touch with what's really important." I was blown away by his insights and realized that my son had become my teacher. I'm glad I asked that question.

■ ■ ■

***If we're open to learning, we can be pleasantly surprised by what our adult children can teach us.***

## Enough is Enough

*F*or Tricia, a mother of two sons in their 30s, the good news was that both of her sons hit bottom, got help and entered recovery from drug and alcohol addictions. The bad news was that, because both had lost everything, they came to live with their mom after they completed treatment.

As she watched her sons slowly self-destruct, Tricia had prayed that they would eventually find their way to sobriety. After losing their families, their careers and their homes, six months apart they arrived on her doorstep. She was able to intervene, making the provision of a safe haven contingent on their completing treatment. This mom got her miracle—she got her sons back. But then they wouldn't leave.

"One's been with me for almost a year and the other for six months. They only work when they feel like it; they eat everything in sight; and they don't pick up their stuff," Tricia told me. "They're pleasant enough; they go to their meetings and buy their own cigarettes, but I feel like I'm living with teenagers." When I responded, "It sounds as though your sons may have worn out their welcome," she exclaimed, "I've turned the welcome mat over now, and on the other side it says, 'Goodbye!'"

Tricia realized that she was nearly as distressed as she had been before her sons got clean. "I've become a total witch," she told me. She gradually came to terms with the fact that it was time to give both sons a move-out deadline, despite the guilt and fear she felt at the prospect. I reassured her that she had given them a great start on their recoveries and that she was entitled to say, "Enough." Tricia gave her sons three months to find their own place and move out. A year later, they are sober, sharing an apartment and working full-time. They come to their mom's house for dinner about once a week. Tricia is always happy to see them.

■　■　■

*Knowing what our limits are and setting appropriate boundaries are essential tools for mothers of adult children.*

## The Roots of Our "Disease to Please"

*O*ne of the most prevalent issues facing mothers is the need to overindulge our adult children by bailing them out of self-imposed financial and relationship messes. Even if they are working full time, we often pay for their vacations, car repairs, clothes, overdue rent and credit card bills. One mother explained, "It's simple: I want him to be happy, and it feels really good to make him happy and really bad to tell him 'No'."

The article entitled "The Good Wife's Guide," from the May, 1955 issue of Good Housekeeping, reminds me of the caretaking legacy I received as I watched my mother serve my father. To help wives keep their husbands happy, the article suggested:

- Have a delicious dinner ready for him—this is the warm welcome he needs.

- Clear away the clutter. Catering to his comfort is immensely satisfying.

- Prepare the children. Have them wash up and encourage them to be quiet.

- Greet him with a warm smile. Show sincerity in your desire to please him.

- Have him sit in his comfy chair. Speak in a low, soothing voice.

- Remember that his topics of conversation are more important than yours.

- He is the master of the house—a good wife always knows her place.

Although we are much less subservient now, it's no wonder that today's women still naturally fall into the role of making things easier for their loved ones.

■ ■ ■

*Although we still have a way to go, there is no question that today's mothers have come a long way, baby!*

# · Epilogue ·

Shortly before writing this final section, my client Emily, whom I hadn't seen for many months, came in for a "check-up from the neck up." When I first met this attorney and mother of Jen, a professional in her own right now in her late thirties, Emily was chronically worried about how irresponsible her daughter was. In addition, their relationship was strained by this mom's critical and controlling communications in the name of "just trying to help."

Motivated by yearning for Jen to want to spend time with her, Emily became a willing student and worked hard in therapy to learn how to face her fears and let go of that which she could not control. In time, this mom lost less sleep, and her relationship with her daughter improved, too.

That afternoon in my office, Emily made one little offhand comment that really made my day. She had come in with a specific situation she hoped I could help her explore but also wanted to update me about her life in general. After sharing mostly good news about her full and rich life, she moved on to her relationship with her daughter, Jen's husband, *and* their little child.

As she calmly described situations of serious procrastination, missed deadlines and dodged bill collectors, with possible consequences ranging from foreclosure to loss of livelihood, I realized that Jen had changed very little. I knew that most mothers would be tearing their hair out if they knew of such circumstances in their adult children's lives. Emily, on the other hand, spoke quietly throughout her report, while a little half-smile graced her face.

When she finished, I asked her how she was doing with all of this, and that's when Emily spoke those spontaneous magic words: Maintaining her bemused countenance and gently shrugging her shoulders, she said with a chuckle and lightness in her voice, "Ah, Jen is just a mystery to me, I guess." That one comment demonstrated the healing that occurs when mothers do their work. Emily had learned to detach, let go of what she could not control and lighten up.

This reflection both made my day and helped me crystallize **my central message to you dear readers: In order to be at peace, we mothers must strive for acceptance *and* for being comfortable with the way things**

**are, rather than how we wish they could be.** Life is indeed messy, and the more we keep our expectations in line with reality, the more content we will feel with our adult children and ourselves. We must hang in there, take responsibility for our distress and, whenever possible, stay connected.

One final recommendation is that you **work hard to remain patient, gentle, kind and forgiving toward yourself.** After many years of working on self-improvement, most of the time I am blessed with that paradoxical grace of feeling both close to and lovingly detached from my children, their partners and kids.

However, both my family relationships and I are still far from perfect. At times, I still step on toes, stick my nose in where it doesn't belong, miss subtle pleas for help, push too hard or give unsolicited advice. Now that my grandchildren are growing up, I have a whole new generation to try and control! I am a much-improved version of myself, however, and, when I recognize these old, familiar patterns, **I do my best to learn from my mistakes. I laugh gently at myself. I accept that things will never be perfect.** I know I will always be a work in progress.

Finally, if you liked what you read here, I invite you to **look for the publication of Volume II of *I Thought I'd Be Done by Now*, scheduled for release early in 2014.** As you continue to walk along your path, my sincere wish is that you be blessed by the peace that radiates from the total acceptance of what is real and true.

# · Index ·

## Topic Reference for Volume I
### *I Thought I'd Be Done by Now*

# · Bibliography ·

Adams, Jane, *I'm Still Your Mother: How to Get Along with Your Grown-up Children for the Rest of Your Life*, iUniverse.com, 2001.

Adams, Jane, *When Our Grown Children Disappoint Us: Letting Go of Their Problems, Loving Them Anyway, and Getting on with Our Lives*, Simon and Schuster, 2003.

Apter, Terri, *The Myth of Maturity: What Teenagers Need from Parents to Become Adults*, W.W. Norton and Company, 2001.

Beattie, Melody, *The Language of Letting Go*, Hazelden Press, 1996.

Borysenko, Joan, *Guilt Is the Teacher, Love Is the Lesson*, Warner Books, 1990.

Bottke, Allison, *Setting Boundaries with Your Adult Children: Six Steps to Hope and Healing for Struggling Parents*, Harvest House Publishers, 2008.

Brach, Tara, *Radical Acceptance: Embracing Your Life with the Heart of a Buddha*, Bantam Books, 2004.

Brown, Brene, *Daring Greatly: How the Courage to Be Vulnerable Transforms the Way We Live, Love, Parent, and Lead*, Penguin Group, 2012.

Brown, Brene, *The Gifts of Imperfection: Let Go of Who You Think You're Supposed to Be and Embrace Who You Are*, Hazelden Press, 2010.

Coburn, Karen and Treeger, Madge, *Letting Go (5th Edition): A Parent's Guide to Understanding the College Years*, Harper Collins, 2009.

Coleman, Joshua, *When Parents Hurt: Compassionate Strategies When You and Your Grown Child Don't Get Along*, Harper Collins, 2008.

Germer, Christopher, *The Mindful Path to Self-Compassion: Freeing Yourself from Destructive Thoughts and Emotions*, Guilford Press, 2009.

Golomb, Elan, *Trapped in the Mirror: Adult Children of Narcissists in Their Struggle for Self*, William Morrow and Company, 1992.

Hendrix, Harville and Hunt, Helen, *Giving the Love that Heals: A Guide for Parents*, Atria Books, 1997.

Kegan, Robert, *The Evolving Self: Problem and Process in Human Development*, Harvard College, 1982.

Maisel, Roberta, *All Grown Up: Living Happily Ever After with Your Adult Children*, New Society Publishers, 2001.

McMeekin, Gail, *The 12 Secrets of Highly Creative Women*, Conari Press, 2000.

McNally, David, *Even Eagles Need a Push: Learning to Soar in a Changing World*, Dell Publishing, 1994.

Muller, Wayne, *A Life of Being Having, and Doing Enough*, Harmony Books, 2010.

Muller, Wayne, *Sabbath: Finding Rest, Renewal, and Delight in Our Busy Lives*, Bantam Books, 1999.

Napthali, Sarah, *Buddhism for Mothers: A Calm Approach to Caring for Yourself and Your Children*, Inspired Living Press, 2003.

Nemzoff, Ruth, *Don't Bite Your Tongue: How to Foster Rewarding Relationships with your Adult Children*, St. Martin's Press, 2008

Peck, Scott, *The Road Less Traveled, 25th Anniversary Edition: A New Psychology of Love, Traditional Values and Spiritual Growth*, Simon and Schuster, 2003.

Pipher, Mary, *The Shelter of Each Other: Rebuilding Our Families*, Ballantine, 2008.

Remen, Rachel Naomi, *My Grandfather's Blessings: Stories of Strength, Refuge, and Belonging*, Riverhead Books, 2000.

Robinson, Anne, *Memoir of an Unfit Mother*, Pocket Books, 2004.

Twenge, Jean, *Generation Me: Why Today's Young Americans Are More Confident, Assertive, Entitled – and More Miserable than Ever Before*, Free Press, 2007.

Sheff, David, *Beautiful Boy: A Father's Journey through His Son's Addiction*, Marriner Books, 2009.

Tannen, Deborah, *You're Wearing That? Understanding Mothers and Daughters in Conversation*, Random House, 2006.

Van Zant, Iyanla, *Peace from Broken Pieces: How to Get Through What You're Going Through*, Smiley Books, 2012.

# · About the Author ·

Wendy Boorn received her Bachelor's degree in English from Bucknell University in 1967. Following graduation, she married, moved across the country, and spent 11 years as a wife and stay-at-home mother of two. Graduate school followed and, in 1980, led to a Master of Counseling degree from Arizona State University.

For thirty-three years, Boorn has worked as a psychotherapist with more than 1,200 adult clients, including hundreds of mid-life parents. In addition, she taught college counseling psychology classes for fifteen years and has developed more than 200 workshops and presentations.

Boorn began her career in the addictions field, where she developed and implemented innovative family treatment programs for eight years. For the last 25 years, she has been the owner of a private psychotherapy practice specializing in transitions, parenting, grief, addiction, and relationship issues. A member of the American Counseling Association and the National Board for Certified Counselors, she is licensed as a Professional Counselor by the Arizona Board of Behavioral Health Examiners.

The author sees herself as a student as well as a teacher and believes that perhaps her greatest asset is an ongoing commitment to her own personal growth. She suspects that it is not just her expertise, but also her humility, sense of humor, and ability to empathize that make her clients want to work hard with her in therapy. She knows that she, and they, are wondrous works in progress, and she infuses her work with this compassion.

Raised in suburban Philadelphia, Boorn now lives in Phoenix, Arizona. Her passions include writing, traveling, playing the piano, creating memory books, and spending time with her grandchildren. On Sundays, she takes time to rest, recreate, and reflect. Living just one mile from her adult daughter, she considers it perhaps her greatest accomplishment that, nearly always, she and her daughter view this proximity as a blessing.